POST KEYNESIAN

MACRODYNAMICS

a more general theory

Michael A. Salant

First Edition 1982
Current printing (last digit): 9 8 7 6 5 4 3 2 1

Typeset in the United States of America by
Monotype Composition Company, Inc.
2050 Rockrose Avenue
Baltimore, Maryland 21211

Printed and bound in the United States of America by
Edwards Brothers, Inc.
2500 South State Street
Post Office Box 1007
Ann Arbor, Michigan 48106

Library of Congress Catalog Card Number: 82-99901
Post Keynesian Macrodynamics: A More General Theory
Salant, Michael Alan
MACRO: economics
Subject matter category: Economic Theory
International Standard Book Number: 0-9609288-0-4 (paperback)
International Standard Book Number: 0-9609288-1-2 (hardbound)

POST KEYNESIAN

MACRODYNAMICS

a more general theory

What This Book is About

The premise of this book is that the standard Keynesian framework, relied on by every economist, has serious deficiencies.

The aim of this book is to present an alternative macroeconomic theory by which stagnation and inflation may be studied in domestic and international contexts.

About the Author-Publisher

Michael A. Salant received his B.A. in mathematics from Harvard College in 1964 and his Ph.D. in economics from Stanford University in 1973. At Stanford he studied international finance and monetary theory and wrote his dissertation on "A Strategy for Operating the Upper Pampanga Irrigation Project: A Case Study in Dynamic Optimization Involving Risk." Since leaving Stanford, Dr. Salant has worked as an international economist for the U. S. Department of the Treasury, as a macro economist for the Economics and Statistics Service of the U. S. Department of Agriculture, and as an independent consultant. From 1964 to 1966, as a member of the Peace Corps, he taught mathematics and educational statistics at Bicol Teachers College, near Legaspi City, in the Philippines. He is a member of American Economic Association, COSMEP (The International Association of Independent Publishers), and The Washington Book Publishers.

Dedication

TO MY PARENTS

Epigraph 1

I've never met a Phi Beta Kappa, a Magna cum Laude, or a Most Likely to Succeed who really made it in life. Sure they made it in some corporate level or in advertising, but they just bit for the old USA oakey-doke and remained oblivious to the realities of what life is actually about.

The great Ringolevio players of my time all made it *in their own ways*—a few went to the electric chair or did terms. Some were great crooks, burglars and stick-up artists but never con men, gangsters or pimps. Others became great athletes, soldiers, radicals, cops, poets and even businessmen. They made it because they learned that you have to move fast in this world. None of them ever got hit by streetcars or automobiles or slipped on banana peels. They were always the ones who caught the ball that was hit into the bleachers and were never the apples who got hit on the head.

Fragment of a quote by Albie Baker, the Greatest Ringolevio Player to Come Out of the Bronx, from *Ringolevio: A Life Played for Keeps* by Emmett Grogan. Copyright © 1972 by Eugene Leo Michael Emmett Grogan. Reprinted by permission of Little, Brown and Company.

Epigraph 2

Do not be defeated by the
Feeling that there is too much for you to know. That
Is a myth of the oppressor. You are
Capable of understanding life. And it is yours alone
And only this time. Someone who excites you
Should be told so, and loved, if you can, but no one
Should be able to shake you so much that you wish to
Give up.

Fragment from "Some General Instructions" from *The Art of Love*, Poems by Kenneth Koch. Copyright © 1972, 1974, 1975 by Kenneth Koch. Reprinted by permission of Vintage Books, a division of Random House.

Epigraph 3

In 1935 an academic scribbler penned the preface to his latest work:

. . . if orthodox economics is at fault, the error is to be found not in the superstructure, which has been erected with great care for logical consistency, but in a lack of clearness and of generality in the premisses.

From *The General Theory of Employment, Interest, and Money* by John Maynard Keynes. Reprinted by permission of Harcourt Brace Jovanovich, Inc.

Abbreviations Used Throughout the Book

FA or FA's means financial assets.

1C means one-country and one-currency. It refers to both a type of world and to the model with no fiscal policy.

3C means three-country and three-currency. It refers to both a type of world and to the international model.

1C(F) refers to the one-country, one-currency model extended to include fiscal policy.

RHS means right-hand side. It refers to one type of equilibrium solution.

LHS means left-hand side. It refers to the other type of equilibrium solution.

The names of model variables are defined on the indicated pages:

For the 1C model: 52–53.

For the 3C model: 86–91.

For the 1C(F) model: 127–129.

For possible extensions of the 1C and 3C models to cover wages: 152.

Table of Contents

Preface

At the present time, economists seem unable to agree how the macroeconomic puzzle fits together. I believe that the current disputes about "philosophy" or practical policy alternatives are symptoms that generally accepted macroeconomic theory is defective. What is needed is a theoretical framework for thinking about macroeconomic issues which aids, rather than confounds, thoughtful analysis.

This book is written in the belief that Keynes' own theory is at fault for one of the very reasons he cited (in the excerpt quoted above) as a failing for the classical (i.e., pre-Keynesian) theory, a lack of generality in the premises.

Keynes' theory assumes an essentially static framework in which the expected rate of inflation is constant, rather than a more general dynamic framework in which the expected rate of inflation might change. Keynes was right that underemployment equilibrium is possible, but the financial side of his model is incomplete and wrong.

Incomplete because it omits explicit treatment of the rate of inflation, real interest rates, the supply of bonds, and makes no attempt to relate short-term and long-term interest rates.

Wrong because it is inconsistent in a dynamic framework, having no posited relationship between real physical saving, the average price level, and nominal financial saving.

In other words, the premise of this book is that the standard Keynesian framework, relied on by every economist, has serious deficiencies.

- It omits many relevant variables.
- It is essentially static.
- It does not properly relate physical and financial flows.
- It does not take proper and full account of the dimensions of its variables.
- It does not properly handle financial stocks and flows.
- It does not usefully relate real output and the price level.
- It is useless for analyzing inflation/deflation.
- It is useless for studying international adjustment, devaluations, and the like.

This book presents an alternative macroeconomic theory to

Keynes' "General Theory" by which stagnation and inflation may be studied in domestic and international contexts. Post Keynesian Macrodynamics is my attempt to piece together in a simple and coherent way the views to which I was exposed while at Stanford University.

This new framework is presented in the form of 12 numerical examples derived from three "back-of-the-envelope" models. Much of the pedagogic value of the book lies in the numerical examples, which are not summarized in words. The reader should work these examples through carefully with a pocket calculator.

The theory which these models embody is more general than Keynes' in the following senses.

• The model is a dynamic model.

• The model is (except for the labor market) an equilibrium model with two possible solutions. There is no labor market equilibrium, because the model has no supply of labor function, a defect the present theory shares with Keynesian theory.

• There are two types of FA's (financial assets), money and perpetual bonds, representing short-term and long-term FA's, respectively.

• The demand for and supply of money and perpetual bonds are defined in terms of real stocks.

• Interest rates are analyzed in real and nominal, and short-term and long-term terms.

• The nominal short-term interest rate is related to the nominal long-term interest rate by an arbitrage condition.

• The allocation of the public's financial holdings between real stocks of money and real stocks of perpetual bonds depends on its portfolio preferences.

• The total real (i.e., deflated or purchasing power) size of the public's financial portfolio of stocks of money and stocks of perpetual bonds depends on real output and the real short-term interest rate.

• The stock demand for the sum of real money plus real perpetual bonds is an increasing function of real output and the real short-term interest rate.

• The stock demand for and stock supply of real money in each currency are equal.

• The stock demand for and stock supply of real perpetual bonds in each currency are equal.

• The nominal value of the flow of real physical saving equals the value of the flow of nominal financial saving.

• Expectations of price changes and exchange rate changes equal the actual (realized) changes.

• The stock supply of nominal money at the start of the period plus the increase in the stock supply of nominal money during the period equals the stock supply of nominal money at the end of the period.

• The annual nominal dividend stream from perpetual bonds at the start of the period plus the increase in the annual nominal dividend stream from perpetual bonds during the period equals the annual nominal dividend stream from perpetual bonds at the end of the period.

It seems to me that the questions the model raises, even about its own adequacy, are the right ones. Thinking about these questions adds to insight, lessens one's confusion, and clarifies thought. This is what a model ought to do, be a tool for easier thinking.

Michael Alan Salant

Washington, D.C.
November 12, 1982

Acknowledgments

I am pleased to acknowledge permission to quote from the following sources:

Ringolevio: A Life Played for Keeps by Emmett Grogan. Copyright © 1972 by Eugene Leo Michael Emmett Grogan. Reprinted by permission of Little, Brown and Company.

The Art of Love, Poems by Kenneth Koch. Copyright © 1972, 1974, 1975 by Kenneth Koch. Reprinted by permission of Vintage Books, a division of Random House.

From *The General Theory of Employment, Interest, and Money* by John Maynard Keynes. Reprinted by permission of Harcourt Brace Jovanovich, Inc.

I am grateful to the U.S. Department of Agriculture for permission to use text and programs that went into some of the early drafts. The views expressed are those of the author and not necessarily those of any government agency.

I would especially like to thank Freeman Dyke, Jr., for his encouragement and assistance when I was starting this project.

I am grateful to Helene Raubitschek, who typed some of the preliminary disks, and to Jan Johnson and Bill Bloom, who taught me to use the Xmark word processor.

I would like to thank Doug Karczewski, Susan Strathmeyer, Jerry Henwood and the people from Speakeasy Computing Corporation, USDA Data Services Center, DPC Corporation, Xmark Mid-Atlantic Corporation, American Management Systems, Martin Marietta Data Systems, and Dial-Tyme for smoothing the path to WYLBUR™. (WYLBUR is a trademark of The Board of Trustees of The Leland Stanford Junior University.)

I would like to thank Betty Marks and Dan Leisher of Monotype Composition Company, Inc., who helped arrange the typesetting and taught me a side of book production that few authors are privileged to learn. I would like to thank Jim Yates, also of Monotype, for executing the figures. I would also like to thank compositors Henry Thomas, Jr., and Bill Fontz of Monotype for making-up a unified and esthetically pleasing book from a rather difficult sequence of art, text, equations, and tables.

I am grateful to Shirley Ellis and Jack Richardson, of Edwards Brothers, Inc., who helped arrange the printing.

I would like to thank Duane Weidman, Charles Sobel, Bill Kramer, Joe Pechman, Roland Hoover, Don Goldsmith, Joan Jeffri, David Howell Jones, and Edna G. Salant, all of whom offered good and timely advice and/or assistance on production and/or distribution.

I am grateful to Sara Gordon and Richard T. Freeman for comments on portions of the draft and galleys, respectively.

I would like to thank those colleagues and associates who taught me modelling, the Speakeasy™ language, who saw the value of basic research, and who listened responsively to my evolving ideas.

I am particularly grateful to Walter Salant and Edward Shaw for inspiration and instruction.

I would especially like to thank my family and friends for their continued interest and support.

POST KEYNESIAN

MACRODYNAMICS

a more general theory

1
Review of Classical and Keynesian Theory

Before describing the new approach, a brief review of the classical and Keynesian frameworks is in order. The frameworks in this review follow the systems of equations in the standard text "Macroeconomic Theory" by Gardner Ackley (page 403).

1. Review of Classical Theory

The nominal interest rate is determined in the classical framework by the intersection of the schedules for real saving and real investment. Real saving is an increasing function of the nominal interest rate. Real investment is a decreasing function of the nominal interest rate. Thus, in the classical equilibrium, the nominal interest rate, real saving, and real investment are simultaneously determined. (See Figure 1.)

The real wage rate is determined in the classical framework by the intersection of the schedules for the demand for labor and the supply of labor. The real wage rate offered to labor, the marginal product of labor, is a decreasing function of employment. The real wage asked for by labor is an increasing function of employment. Real output is an increasing function of employment. Thus, in the classical equilibrium, the real wage rate, employment, and real output are simultaneously determined. (See Figure 2.)

The stock demand for real money in the classical framework (Figure 3) is an increasing function of real output.

1

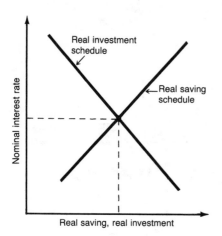

Figure 1 Determination of the nominal interest rate, real saving, and real investment in the classical framework.

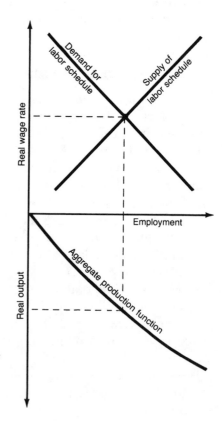

Figure 2 Determination of the real wage rate, employment, and real output in the classical framework.

Figure 3 Determination of the stock demand for real money in the classical framework.

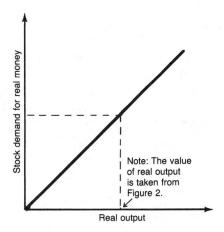

Note: The value of real output is taken from Figure 2.

The stock supply of nominal money determines the price level and the nominal wage rate in the classical framework. In fact, any one of the above variables determines the other two. The chain proceeds as follows. The stock supply of nominal money and the stock supply of real money determine the price level. The price level and the real wage rate determine the nominal wage rate. (See Figure 4a.)

If the nominal wage rate were given, it and the real wage rate would determine the price level. Then the price level and the stock supply of real money would determine the stock supply of nominal money. (See Figure 4b.)

If the price level were given, it and the real wage rate would determine the nominal wage rate, and it and the stock supply of real money would determine the stock supply of nominal money. Recall that the real wage rate is determined by the supply and demand for labor, which result also determines real output, which in turn determines the stock demand for real money, which, in equilibrium, equals the stock supply of real money. (See Figure 4c.)

2. Review of Keynesian Theory

The Keynesian framework may be simply viewed in terms of the IS-LM diagram, which summarizes the relationships among most of the variables.

The IS-LM diagram in the Keynesian framework (Figure 5) has units of real output on the horizontal axis and the nominal long-term interest rate on the vertical axis.

The IS-LM diagram has two features: the IS curve and the LM curve. The IS curve is derived as follows.

The flow of real (i.e., physical) saving during the period in the Keynesian framework (Figure 6) is an increasing function of real output during the period.

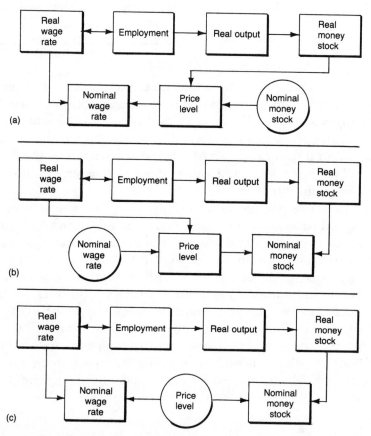

Figures 4a, 4b, 4c   In the classical framework, any one of the following three variables determines the other two: nominal money stock, nominal wage rate, price level.

Note: Circles represent the exogenous variable. Rectangles represent the endogenous variables.

Figure 5   The IS-LM diagram
in the Keynesian framework.

Note: The LM curve also depends
on both the price level and the
stock supply of nominal money.

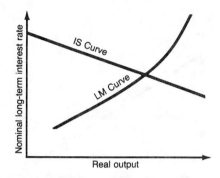

   The flow of real (i.e., physical) investment during the period
in the Keynesian framework (Figure 7) is a decreasing function
of the nominal long-term interest rate. Note that in the
Keynesian framework, the expected rate of inflation appears
implicitly in the real investment function.
   The IS curve in the Keynesian framework (Figure 8) indicates
the combinations of values of the nominal long-term interest
rate and real output for which real saving and real investment
are equal.
   The IS curve slopes from the upper left to the lower right.
At the upper left, where there are high values of the nominal
long-term interest rate and low values of real output, real
investment and real saving are both low. At the lower right,
where there are low values of the nominal long-term interest
rate and high values of real output, real investment and real
saving are both high.

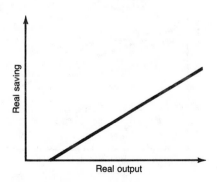

Figure 6   The real saving
schedule in the Keynesian
framework.

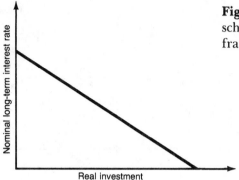

Figure 7   The real investment schedule in the Keynesian framework.

The LM curve is derived as follows. The transactions stock demand for nominal money in the Keynesian framework (Figure 9) is an increasing function of nominal output (i.e., real output times the price level).

The speculative stock demand for nominal money in the Keynesian framework (Figure 10) is a decreasing function of the nominal long-term interest rate.

The LM curve in the Keynesian framework (Figure 11) indicates the combinations of values of the nominal long-term interest rate and real output for which the stock supply of nominal money equals the sum of the transactions stock demand for nominal money and the speculative stock demand for nominal money.

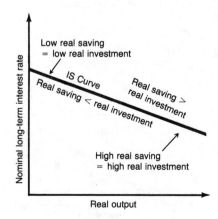

Figure 8   The IS curve in the Keynesian framework.

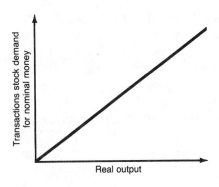

Figure 9   The schedule for the transactions stock demand for nominal money in the Keynesian framework.

Note: The schedule for the transactions stock demand for nominal money also depends on the price level.

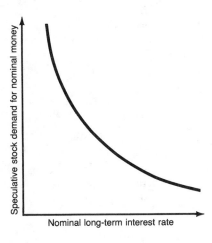

Figure 10   The schedule for the speculative stock demand for nominal money in the Keynesian framework.

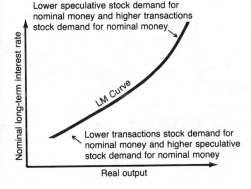

Figure 11   The LM curve in the Keynesian framework.

Note: The LM curve also depends on both the price level and the stock supply of nominal money.

The LM curve slopes from the lower left to the upper right. At the lower left, where there are low values of the nominal long-term interest rate and low values of real output, the speculative stock demand for nominal money is high and the transactions stock demand for nominal money is low. At the upper right, where there are high values of the nominal long-term interest rate and high values of real output, the speculative stock demand for nominal money is low, and the transactions stock demand for nominal money is high.

The flow chart (Figure 12) shows the sequence of computations for a numerical computer model along the lines of the Keynesian framework, derived by the author from the Keynesian system of equations in "Macroeconomic Theory" by Gardner Ackley (page 403).

The solution process in the Keynesian framework begins with an arbitrary nominal wage rate and nominal money supply. A trial value for the nominal long-term interest rate is selected.

Step 1: From the nominal long-term interest rate is found real investment.

Step 2: Real saving equals real investment in equilibrium.

Step 3: From real saving is found real output.

(The previous three steps make use of the curves underlying the IS curve.)

Step 4: From real output is found employment.

Step 5: From employment is found the real wage rate.

Step 6: From the real wage rate and the pre-specified nominal wage rate is found the price level.

Step 7: From the price level and the previously obtained value of real output is found the transactions stock demand for nominal money.

Step 8: From the transactions stock demand for nominal money and the pre-specified stock supply of nominal money is found the speculative stock demand for nominal money.

Step 9: From the speculative stock demand for nominal money is found a (possibly different) value of the nominal long-term interest rate.

(The previous three steps make use of the curves underlying the LM curve.)

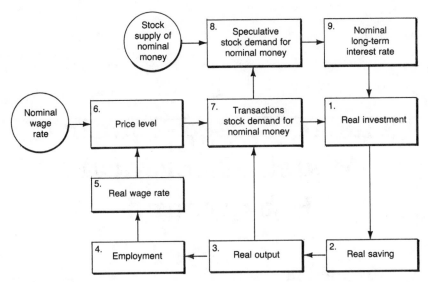

Figure 12   Flow chart for the Keynesian framework.

Note: Circles represent exogenous variables. Rectangles represent endogenous variables. Numbers inside rectangles refer to the steps in the solution process.

The process is repeated until the value of the nominal long-term interest rate at the end of the process is the same value as at the start of the process.

There was also another arrangement of equations, which, for the example tested, produced a spurious solution. This arrangement amounted to starting at Step 6, with an arbitrary value of the price level, and proceeding in reverse order, through Steps 5, . . . , 1, 9, 8, 7, etc. The solution produced was obviously incorrect, because the nominal long-term interest rate was negative. However, the fact that the same set of equations may yield two solutions should be kept in mind, because the Post Keynesian Macrodynamic model also yields two solutions. Although I believe that both of them make sense.

2

The 1C Closed-Country Model: Theoretical Background

1. Introduction

Worlds

In the framework of this book there are two types of worlds: a world with one country and one currency (denoted: 1C), and a world with three countries and three currencies (denoted: 3C). In the three-country, three-currency world clear distinctions are made between country and currency variables.

Financial Assets

In each currency there are two types of financial assets: money and perpetual bonds. The public has stock demands for real money and real perpetual bonds, respectively, which it compares with the available stock supplies of real money and real perpetual bonds, respectively. Because the model is an equilibrium model, the public's stock demands always match available stock supplies. If they did not match, a disequilibrium situation would exist and adjustment would occur. (Adjustment to disequilibrium is discussed in Appendix 6.)

The distinction between money and perpetual bonds is as follows. Money has a constant nominal principal value but a variable annual payment that depends on the nominal short-term interest rate, IST. The stock supply of nominal money, MS, is measured in dollars. The magnitude of the variable MS

10

may be thought of as the number of money units having a constant nominal principal value of one dollar. The stock supply of real money equals MS/P.

Perpetual bonds have a constant annual nominal dividend (or coupon), but a variable price or capitalized nominal market value that depends on the nominal long-term interest rate, ILT. The annual nominal dividend stream (that is, the instantaneous annual rate of nominal coupon flow) from perpetual bonds, DS, is measured in dollars per year. The magnitude of the variable DS may usefully be thought of as the number of perpetual dividend stream units paying a constant nominal flow of one dollar per year forever, even though in reality these bonds may have been issued at many different prevailing interest rates. Note that the nominal market price of a single perpetual bond paying one dollar per year forever is (100/ILT). The stock supply of real perpetual bonds equals $((100 * DS)/(ILT * P))$, in other words the deflated value of the capitalized annual nominal dividend stream from perpetual bonds.

The amount of the net change in the nominal money supply during the period equals the nominal value of that money net newly issued during the period. Money may be issued during the period through four different mechanisms: (1) money may be issued to finance capital formation by the private sector (i.e., real investment); (2) money may be printed to finance the government budget deficit; (3) money may be sold in the course of central bank money-bond operations in the domestic currency; (4) domestic money may be sold in the course of central bank foreign exchange operations (i.e., domestic money-foreign money operations).

The amount of the net change in the annual nominal dividend stream from perpetual bonds during the period (i.e., the amount of the net change in the instantaneous annual rate of nominal coupon flow from perpetual bonds during the period) equals the annual nominal dividend stream from those perpetual bonds net newly issued during the period. Perpetual bonds may be issued during the period through three different mechanisms: (1) bonds may be issued to finance capital formation by the private sector (i.e., real investment); (2) bonds may be printed to finance the government budget deficit; (3) bonds may be sold in the course of central bank money-bond operations in the domestic currency.

Changes in the nominal money supply or the annual nominal dividend stream from perpetual bonds during the period are on a net basis (i.e., net of any redemptions that might occur).

Goods

The world contains a single type of physical good, which is tradable with zero transport costs, storable with zero storage costs, durable, and which, when used as a capital good, does not depreciate. Therefore, gross investment and net investment are equal, as are gross output and net output. There is no effect on real output or real saving from any change in the capital stock resulting from net investment. There is no explicit role for the capital stock. There is no physical production function for converting inputs to outputs.

The good is produced, consumed, and used as the investment good (i.e., for capital to produce more of itself) in each country, traded (i.e., imported and exported from current production), and exchanged (i.e., bought and sold from earlier production).

Because the model is an equilibrium model, *ex ante* and *ex post* real saving are always equal, as are *ex ante* and *ex post* real investment.

There is no breakdown of investment into fixed investment and inventory investment. Therefore, there is no distinction between final sales and inventories.

Time

Time is discrete in the model; that is, time is measured in periods. There are two types of "location in time":

a. points in time which define the beginning or ends of periods (example: midnight on New Year's Eve).

b. intervals in time which are the periods thus defined (example: the calendar year itself). The phrases "during the period" or "over the period" refer to these intervals in time.

Production of goods and creation and destruction of financial assets (i.e., money and bonds) normally take place during periods. Goods produced and money and/or bonds created (or destroyed) during the current period are referred to as "new". Goods produced and money and/or bonds created in previous periods (and still existing) are referred to as "old".

Nominal and real stocks of money and perpetual bonds are measured at the start of a period (which is the end of the previous period).

The price level, the nominal long-term interest rate, and exchange rates may be measured at two times:

a. at the start of a period (the end of the previous period).

b. during the period or over the period (as an average).

Formulas for changes in price levels and exchange rates assume that the changes are discrete.

The convention is followed that the variables ILT, ILTNXT, ILTAVG, IST, RLT, RST, PDOT, PDOTE, KDOT, KDOTE, HDOT, and HDOTE are expressed in percent, not as decimals.

The subjective expectations for the variables PDOTE, KDOTE, HDOTE are formed at the start of the period.

Institutions

The model assumes that foreign exchange operations are handled by a single world-level central bank exchange authority which has unlimited inventories of money in each of the three currencies and can buy or sell money in any currency in any amount in order to maintain a balance of supply of and demand for each money at any specified exchange rate.

The model assumes that domestic money-bond operations are handled by the three national central bank monetary authorities, each of which has unlimited inventories of money and bonds in its home currency.

These intervention operations may be undertaken in order to affect either the relative price of the objects exchanged or their relative quantities. Central bank money-bond operations may be undertaken to affect either the nominal long-term interest rate (the relative price) or the relative quantities of money and bonds outstanding. Central bank foreign exchange operations may be undertaken to affect either the exchange rate between the two currencies or the relative quantities of money outstanding in the two currencies. In each case, intervention could be undertaken either to cause a change viewed by the authorities as desirable or to offset or prevent a change viewed by the authorities as undesirable.

In the 1C(F) model (see below), the fiscal operations are done by the Treasury.

Models

There are three models that will be simulated:

1. A one-country, one-currency model *with no fiscal policy* (the 1C model) showing applications to economic policy, including alternative targeting of the money supply, the nominal long-term interest rate, or the nominal short-term interest rate. The 1C model is set forth in Chapters 2–4 and exemplified in Simulations 1–5.

2. A three-country, three-currency model *with no fiscal policy* (the 3C model) showing applications to floating exchange rates, fixed (and constant) exchange rates, and two examples of devaluations under fixed exchange rates. The 3C model permits analysis of global macroeconomic interactions and international payments accounts. The 3C model does not employ the small country assumption. The 3C model is set forth in Chapters 5–6 and exemplified in Simulations 6–9.

3. A one-country, one-currency model *with fiscal policy* (the 1C(F) model) including budget deficits. Fiscal policy comprises taxation, government purchases, government deficit financing, and government debt servicing. The 1C(F) model is set forth in Chapter 7 and exemplified in Simulations 10–12.

All three models have an explicit monetary policy.

Notation

Many of the formulas follow the conventions of the computer language FORTRAN.

In algebra, variables usually have names consisting of one letter, such as X or Y. In FORTRAN, variable names must begin with a letter but may be up to 6 alphanumeric characters in length. Thus, INVRL, Q, MSNXT, ILTAVG, PDOTE, and RST are all valid names for variables in FORTRAN.

Many of the variables in the model have names which contain mnemonic groupings of letters which are designed to make it a little easier to recall the characteristics of the particular variables. Examples of these mnemonics are: NL (nominal), RL (real), ST (short-term), LT (long-term), NX or NXT (end-of-period, start-of-next-period), DEL (net change during period), DOT (actual rate of change over period), DOTE (expected rate of change over period), and AV or AVG (average over period). In addition, in the 3C (international) model, the variable names have suffixes of A, B, or C, which refer to either country or currency.

The various mathematical operations are indicated as follows:

1. square roots by the intrinsic function DSQRT;
2. natural logarithms by the intrinsic function DLOG;
3. exponentiation by two asterisks in a row;
4. multiplication by a single asterisk;
5. division by a slash;
6. addition by a plus sign;
7. subtraction by a minus sign.

If there are not enough parentheses to clarify the order of computation, the FORTRAN hierarchies prevail: functions first, exponentiation second, multiplication and division third, addition and subtraction fourth; in case of ties, the operations go from left to right, except for exponentiation which goes from right to left.

The geometric mean is used to compute the average value during the period from the values at the start and the end of the period for the following variables: P, ILT, K, H, WNL, WRL, NDMS, NDDS. The geometric mean of two positive numbers is the positive square root of their product.

The reader will note that consumption, imports, and exports are seldom mentioned explicitly. Using the concepts of output, saving, and investment (and in the fiscal model, government purchases and tax revenues), it is possible to deal with consumption, imports and exports without explicitly mentioning them. For example, in the 3C model the real trade balance for a country equals real saving for the country less real investment for the country.

2. The IS-FA Diagram

The Post Keynesian Macrodynamic model is a complex and highly interrelated system of equations. Nevertheless, the basic ideas may be easily gotten across by means of two diagrams and an equation which connects them. The first diagram (discussed in this section) is the IS-FA diagram. The second diagram (discussed in Section 5) is the money-bonds diagram. The variables in the IS-FA diagram and the money-bonds diagram are connected by the linking equation (discussed in Section 3).

The variables of the 1C model are listed and defined in Section 2 of Chapter 4.

The IS-FA diagram (Figure 13) has units of Q, real output during the period, on the two (identical) horizontal axes; RLT, the real long-term interest rate, start of period, on the upper vertical axis; and RST, the real short-term interest rate, start of period, on the lower vertical axis. In the IS-FA diagram, RLT has a positive upper limit, and RST has a negative lower limit. RST cannot be less than -100 (otherwise the stock demand for real FA's would be negative). Also, RLT cannot exceed 87.5 percent (otherwise real investment would be negative).

The IS-FA diagram has two features: the IS curve and the FA-curve field, which is a field of stock iso-demand curves for real FA's.

The IS curve is derived as follows.

The flow of real (i.e., physical) saving during the period in the Post Keynesian Macrodynamic framework (Figure 14) is an increasing function of real output during the period. In the 1C model the equation for the flow of physical saving is:

$$SAVRL = -5 + .1 * Q.$$

The flow of real (i.e., physical) investment during the period in the Post Keynesian Macrodynamic framework (Figure 15) is

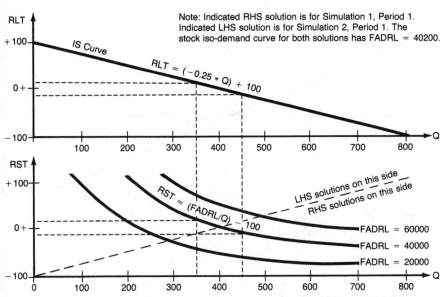

Figure 13 The IS-FA diagram in the Post Keynesian Macrodynamic framework.

Note: Because there is a one-to-one correspondence between real output and employment, each level of real output determines a corresponding level of employment.

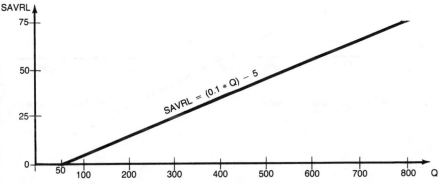

Figure 14 The real saving schedule in the Post Keynesian Macrodynamic framework.

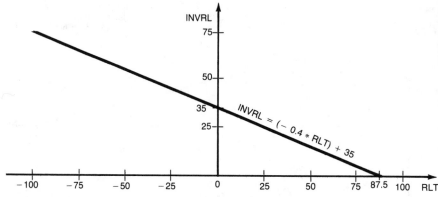

Figure 15   The real investment schedule in the Post Keynesian Macrodynamic framework.

a decreasing function of the real long-term interest rate at the start of the period. In the 1C model the equation for the flow of physical investment is:

$$INVRL = 35 - .4 * RLT.$$

The IS curve in the Post Keynesian Macrodynamic framework (Figure 16) indicates the combinations of values of the real

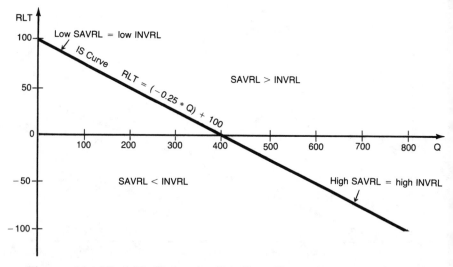

Figure 16   The IS Curve in the Post Keynesian Macrodynamic framework.

long-term interest rate at the start of the period, RLT, and real output during the period, Q, for which real saving during the period and real investment during the period are equal. In the 1C model the equation for the IS curve is:

$$RLT = 100 - .25 * Q.$$

The IS curve slopes from the upper left to the lower right. At the upper left, where there are high values of the real long-term interest rate and low values of real output, real investment and real saving are both low. At the lower right, where there are low values of the real long-term interest rate and high values of real output, real investment and real saving are both high.

The field of stock iso-demand curves for real FA's shows the stock demand of the public for real FA's that exists for each combination of values of the real short-term interest rate, RST, and real output, Q. The field of stock iso-demand curves for real FA's is derived as follows.

The stock demand for real financial assets in the Post Keynesian Macrodynamic framework (Figure 17) is an increasing function of both the real short-term interest rate at the start of the period, RST, and real output during the period, Q. In the 1C model the equation for the stock demand for real (i.e., deflated) financial assets is:

$$FADRL = Q * (RST + 100).$$

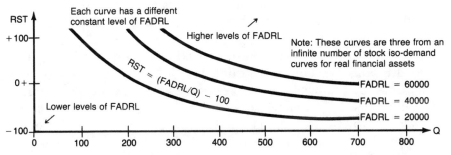

Figure 17 The field of stock iso-demand curves for real financial assets (or real FA demand curve field) in the Post Keynesian Macrodynamic framework.

The value of 100 in the stock demand function for real FA's is arbitrary.

The stock iso-demand curves for real FA's connect pairs of values of real output, Q, and the real short-term interest rate, RST, which have equal stock demands for real FA's, FADRL.

The stock iso-demand curves for real FA's by country are rectangular hyperbolas asymptotic to axes of $Q = 0.0$ and $RST = -100$, each member of which corresponds to a different real FA stock demand (FADRL) for the country:

$$RST = (FADRL/Q) - 100.$$

This choice is for illustration only, the purpose being to produce convex stock iso-demand curves.

The justification of the stock demand function for real FA's is that the public measures its holdings of money plus bonds in real (i.e., deflated) terms and that its desired holdings increase with the level of real (i.e., physical) production and also with the real interest return (i.e., after inflation) on money.

Other choices of variables are possible. Instead of real output, it would be possible to use private consumption, total domestic expenditure, or disposable income (and, perhaps, real stocks of physical goods as well). Instead of the real short-term interest rate it would be possible to use two variables, the nominal short-term interest rate and the expected rate of inflation.

Note that the real short-term interest rate in the stock demand function for real FA's is the real interest rate on money holdings and bonds (if capital gains and losses are included), not on goods, after the effect of inflation has been removed. It is the rate of increase in the purchasing power value of the FA's.

Holders of money and bonds look upon FA's as claims on present or future output, as forms other than goods in which wealth may be held. In order for savers to be willing to accumulate financial claims to output rather than output itself, savers must be convinced that the real value of their financial claims in the future will make it worthwhile to forgo purchasing output in the present.

The flow of real saving (from production) is an increasing function of the nominal interest rate in the classical framework, but an increasing function of real output (or real disposable income) in both the Keynesian and the Post Keynesian Macro-dynamic frameworks.

In the Post Keynesian Macrodynamic framework, it is the stock demand for real financial assets—not the flow of real saving—which is an increasing function of the real short-term interest rate.

3. The Linking Equation

This section introduces the linking equation.

The saving-investment process involves the creation or issuing of new money and/or new perpetual bonds by investors and the creation or production of more real output by savers than the savers want to consume. The savers sell the excess real output to the investors and acquire in return the new money and/or new perpetual bonds created by the investors.

The linking equation in the Post Keynesian Macrodynamic framework equates the value of the flow of nominal financial saving during the period and the nominal value of the flow of real physical saving during the period. The former is equal to the nominal value of money plus perpetual bonds (net) newly issued during the period. The latter equals real saving times the average price level during the period.

In the 1C model the linking equation is:

$$MSDEL + BDEL = SAVRL * PAVG.$$

(Note: Both sides of this equation equal SAVNL.)

When divided by PAVG, the linking equation says that real saving (i.e., production that is not consumed) during the period, equals the deflated value of the nominal value of money and perpetual bonds (net) newly issued during the period.

Note: The linking equation (but not the next two equations) refers only to those new issues of money and perpetual bonds whose creation was due to capital formation, not to those whose creation was due to central bank money-bond operations in the domestic currency, central bank foreign exchange operations, government operations to finance the budget deficit, nor to issues of money and/or perpetual bonds to buy existing goods and/or financial assets (or to distribute *gratis*).

If money and/or perpetual bonds are issued to purchase goods (i.e., physical capital), then the real (i.e., physical) amount of capital purchased in the period when the claims were issued equals the real (i.e., deflated) value of the financial claims issued. In later periods, however, the real value of the claims may diverge from the real value of the capital, because of changes in the price level and/or the nominal long-term interest rate.

The change in nominal bonds during the period refers to the nominal principal value of perpetual bonds (net) newly issued during the period. Note that although the net newly issued perpetual bonds are issued during the period at their par (or face) value, bonds issued during the period may be trading at a discount or premium by the end of the period if long-term nominal interest rates are rising or falling, respectively.

Because all outstanding perpetual bonds compete on the same footing in the market regardless of the nominal long-term interest rate at which they were originally issued, and because the nominal long-term interest rate varies from period to period, the cumulative sum of BDEL over time is not a meaningful way to measure the stock supply of real perpetual bonds.

There are two steps necessary in order to fit new issues of bonds into the framework of the model. First, the total nominal (principal) value of bonds issued during the period must be converted into the change in the annual nominal dividend stream. This is done as follows. The net change during the period in the annual nominal dividend stream from perpetual bonds equals the average nominal long-term interest rate during the period times the nominal principal value of perpetual bonds (net) newly issued during the period.

$$\text{DSDEL} = (\text{ILTAVG}/100) * \text{BDEL}.$$

Second, the change in the annual nominal dividend stream during the period must be used to obtain the end-of-period value for the annual nominal dividend stream. This is done as follows.

$$\text{DSNXT} = \text{DS} + \text{DSDEL}.$$

Note: A bank loan might be represented by the public creating a bond, a bank creating money, and these two claims being exchanged. The money supply of the public is increased as is the bond supply of the bank (which does not enter into the model). With repayment of the loan the money supply declines with the borrower in effect covering his/her short position in money and wiping out the debt.

4. The Money-Dividend Streams Diagram

This section introduces the money-dividend streams diagram, which is used to obtain the nominal long-term interest rate from the portfolio preferences of the public between holdings of money and perpetual bonds.

The manner in which choices are analyzed in economic models is frequently the same, even when the choices differ. Considering two examples, the choice between holding money and bonds and the choice between consuming tea and coffee are fundamentally similar in the sense that both choices involve the maximization of utility subject to a constraint. Both choices must be made at both the micro level (by pairs of individuals) and the macro level (by the entire economy), although the adjustments in the micro and macro levels involve different mechanisms.

If two individuals are dissatisfied with their respective holdings of tea and coffee in a barter economy, they may exchange with each other at the prevailing relative price ratio.

If the public as a whole is dissatisfied with its holdings of tea and coffee in a barter economy, the collective attempt by individuals to swap tea and coffee will result in a change in the relative price ratio in such a manner that the relative price ratio will become tangent to the utility curve passing through the portfolio point representing the public's holdings of tea and coffee.

Using the field of portfolio preference curves and a "macro budget constraint", the public can optimize its portfolio between money and bonds in much the same way as an individual consumer could optimize consumption between tea and coffee.

The nominal price of money is (by definition) equal to one. The relative price of money with respect to perpetual bonds is (ILT/100). The relative price of money with respect to goods is (1/P).

Just as the relative price of tea and coffee varies with their relative quantities, as the relative quantities of money and perpetual bonds shifts, the value of ILT adjusts so as to keep the asset holders at a utility optimum.

If two individuals are dissatisfied with their respective holdings of money and bonds, they may exchange with each other at the prevailing relative price ratio, which is the nominal long-term interest rate.

If the public as a whole is dissatisfied with its holdings of money and bonds, the collective attempt by individuals to swap money and bonds will result in a change in the relative price ratio, which is the nominal long-term interest rate, in such a manner that the relative price ratio will become tangent to the utility curve passing through the portfolio point representing the public's holdings of money and bonds.

The justification of the portfolio preference curves in the money-dividend streams diagram is merely that the public has preferences between holding money and perpetual bonds in the same way that, in another model, it might have preferences between consuming tea and coffee. The situation is not exactly analogous, because tea and coffee are nondurable consumption goods, and their consumption is a flow. In contrast, money is a stock and the dividend streams are perpetual flows. However, one can view the preferences as being between holdings of claims on money and claims on perpetual income streams from perpetual bonds. (And one can also view the utility from such holdings as flows.) Additional differences are that the money-bond choice is not made in a barter economy, and that neither choice (tea-coffee or money-bonds) is presented in an intertemporal framework.

In the next section the focus will shift somewhat from nominal money and nominal dividend streams to real money and real perpetual bonds, with the nominal stocks being deflated by the price level. For a similar treatment of the tea-coffee analogy the real quantities of tea and coffee would have to be not the

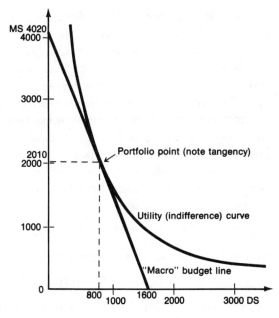

Figure 18   The money-dividend streams diagram in the Post Keynesian Macrodynamic framework.

Note: The portfolio point indicated has the actual values for all 1C and 1C(F) simulations (except Simulation 5) at the start of Period 1.

physical quantities but rather the respective money values of the two goods deflated by the overall price level of the economy.

The money-dividend streams diagram in the Post Keynesian Macrodynamic framework (Figure 18) shows the iso-utility curves and iso-budget lines of all possible portfolios of money and perpetual bonds available to the public.

The money-dividend streams diagram has units of DS, the annual nominal dividend stream from perpetual bonds, start of period, on the horizontal axis and MS, the stock supply of nominal money, start of period, on the vertical axis.

Budget lines on the money-dividend streams diagram connect all portfolios of money and dividend streams which can be purchased by a fixed nominal budget. The slope of the budget line depends on the nominal long-term interest rate, and the MS-intercept is the fixed nominal budget amount.

The field of portfolio preference curves shows the amount of utility to the public afforded by portfolios containing various combinations of nominal money (MS) and annual nominal dividend streams from perpetual bonds (DS). The present utility function omits the price level as a simplification, but that omission does not change the formula for ILT.

Indifference curves on the money-dividend streams diagram connect all portfolios of money and dividend streams which have equal utilities for the public.

The indifference curves of the public between money and perpetual bonds are assumed to be defined by the Cobb-Douglas utility function:

$$U = A * (MS ** B) * (DS **(C - B))$$

which, together with a budget line:

$$FA = MS + (100/ILT) * DS$$

will determine the public's choices of money and bonds for its portfolio.

The slope of the utility curves $= ((B - C) * MS)/(B * DS)$ (which gives Property One below).

The slope of the budget line $= -100/ILT$.

Since the algebraic solution maximizes utility for a fixed budget, the indifference curve and the budget line are tangent and have equal slopes.

By equating the slopes, it follows that at points of tangency:

$$MS/DS = (100 * B)/((C - B) * ILT)$$

and by solving this equation together with the equation for the budget line, it follows that for a budget of FA dollars:

$$MS = (B * FA)/C$$

(which gives Property Two below) and

$$DS = ((ILT * (C - B) * FA)/(100 * C)$$

and also that

$$MS/FA = B/C$$

and

$$DS/FA = (ILT * (C - B))/(100 * C).$$

(Note: In the examples in this book, the ratio B/C is denoted by THETA and assigned an arbitrary value of 0.5.)

Property One: The slopes of the indifference curves are the same along any ray from the origin. (The values of the slopes differ for different rays.)

Property Two: If a line crossing the vertical axis at point A is tangent to an indifference curve at some point B, then every point C on the same horizontal level as point B is also a point of tangency between the indifference curve through C and a line connecting A and C. (Note: Budget lines with equal vertical intercepts on the MS axis have equal nominal budgets.)

Example for the Money-Dividend Streams Diagram:

For this example, as in the model, THETA = 0.50.
(This value of THETA implies that the nominal capitalized value of the dividend stream equals the nominal money supply.)

Case 1: Suppose MS = 150 and DS = 15.

Since ILT = $((DS * THETA)/(MS * (1 - THETA))) * 100$, it follows that ILT = 10.

Case 2: Suppose MS = 150 and DS = 20.

Since ILT = $((DS * THETA)/(MS * (1 - THETA))) * 100$, it follows that ILT = 13.333.

Case 3: Suppose MS = 180 and DS = 15.

Since ILT = $((DS * THETA)/(MS * (1 - THETA))) * 100$, it follows that ILT = 8.333.

Case 4: Suppose MS = 180 and DS = 20.

Since ILT = $((DS * THETA)/(MS * (1 - THETA))) * 100$, it follows that ILT = 11.111.

Since in equilibrium the stock supply of real money equals THETA times the stock demand for real FA's, the income velocity of money = $1/(THETA * (RST + 100))$.

The solutions to the money-dividend streams diagram are more easily put into the framework of the model using the money-bonds diagram, which displays the stock supplies of money and bonds in real terms. The money-bonds diagram is introduced in the next section.

5. The Money-Bonds Diagram

This section introduces the money-bonds diagram, which is used to obtain the price level. Using the money-bonds diagram, it is possible to derive those values of the price level and the nominal long-term interest rate which are consistent with the stock supply of nominal money and the annual nominal dividend stream from perpetual bonds being compatible with the stock demand for real money and the stock demand for real perpetual bonds.

The money-bonds diagram in the Post Keynesian Macrodynamic framework (Figure 19) is a transformation of the money-dividend streams diagram which makes it easier to study the adjustment to portfolio disequilibrium of the price level and the nominal long-term interest rate.

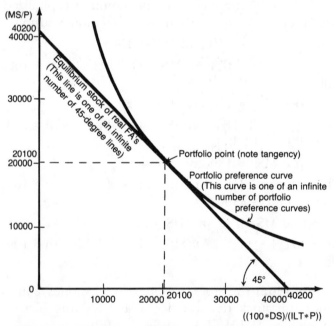

Figure 19 The money-bonds diagram in the Post Keynesian Macro-dynamic framework.

Note: The portfolio point indicated has the actual values for all 1C and 1C(F) simulations (except Simulation 5) at the start of Period 1.

The money-bonds diagram has units of $((100 * DS)/(ILT * P))$, the stock supply of real perpetual bonds, start of period, on the horizontal axis and (MS/P), the stock supply of real money, start of period, on the vertical axis.

The money-bonds diagram has two features: a field of portfolio preference curves of the public (derived from the utility function on the money-dividend streams diagram) and a field of iso-supply lines for real FA's.

The field of portfolio preference curves shows the amount of utility to the public afforded by portfolios containing various combinations of quantities of real money (MS/P) and real perpetual bonds $((100 * DS)/(ILT * P))$.

Each portfolio preference curve in the money-bonds diagram connects portfolios of real money and real bonds which have equal levels of utility for the public.

The field of stock supply curves (negatively sloping 45-degree lines) of real FA's shows the stock supply of real FA's that exists for each possible portfolio of the public containing both real money (MS/P) and real perpetual bonds $((100 * DS)/(ILT * P))$.

Each stock iso-supply line of real FA's in the money-bonds diagram connects portfolios having equal totals of real money plus real bonds. These lines are negatively sloping 45-degree lines. Only a downward sloping 45-degree line has the property that every point on it represents a portfolio of constant real value.

On the money-bonds diagram, the ratio of real money to real bonds in equilibrium is determined by the portfolio preference utility function (which can be summarized by the value of the parameter THETA), and the value of the sum of real money plus real bonds in equilibrium is determined by the real FA stock demand function, which is determined by the particular values of RST and Q. When the total of real money plus real bonds and the ratio of real money to real bonds are both determined, so is the amount of each.

The algebraic and graphic solutions to the constrained maximization problem of Section 4 are not changed by graphing the equations on the money-bonds diagram.

Using the axes of this diagram, the utility function becomes:

$$U = A * (P ** C) * ((ILT/100) ** (C-B)) * ((MS/P) ** B) * (((100 * DS)/(ILT * P)) ** (C-B)),$$

and the budget line becomes:

$$FA = P * (MS/P) + P * ((100 * DS)/(ILT * P)).$$

The slope of the budget line on the new axes is -1, meaning that the slope of the utility curve at points of tangency on the new axes will also be -1.

(Note: In the formulas below, the ratio FA/P is denoted by FADRL.) By transforming the equations in Section 4, it follows that:

$$(MS/P)/((100 * DS)/(ILT * P)) = B/(C - B)$$

and

$$MS/P = (B * FA)/(C * P)$$

and

$$((100 * DS)/(ILT * P)) = ((C-B) * FA)/(C * P)$$

and also that:

$$(MS/P)/(FADRL) = B/C$$

and

$$((100 * DS)/(ILT * P))/(FADRL) = (C - B)/C.$$

From which it follows that:

$$P = (C * MS)/(B * (FADRL))$$

or

$$P = MS/(FADRL * THETA)$$

and

$$ILT = (B * 100 * DS)/((C - B) * MS)$$

or

$$ILT = ((DS * THETA)/(MS * (1 - THETA))) * 100.$$

When graphed with the axes MS and DS of the money-dividend streams diagram, changes in the nominal long-term interest rate affect the budget line but not the indifference curve field.

When graphed with the axes (MS/P) and ((100 * DS)/(ILT * P)) of the money-bonds diagram, changes in the nominal long-term interest rate affect the indifference curve field but not the budget line.

The portfolio preference curves in the money-bonds diagram are transformations of the indifference curves in the money-dividend streams diagram. Each indifference curve from the money-dividend streams diagram is mapped into an infinite number of portfolio preference curves (one for each value of ILT) on the money-bonds diagram. This means that the value of the utility represented by each portfolio preference curve on the money-bonds diagram is a function of the nominal long-term interest rate, ILT, as well as the position of the portfolio point on the diagram, rather than—as on the money-dividend streams diagram—only a function of the position of the portfolio point. This will not cause problems, because the single algebraic solution which underlies both diagrams is not affected.

The algebraic solutions of MS, DS, (MS/P), and ((100 * DS)/(ILT * P)) are independent of the graphic representation. These solutions show that of the four variables above, MS, (MS/P), and ((100 * DS)/(ILT * P)) are independent of the nominal long-term interest rate and depend only on the budget constraint and the parameter THETA, whereas DS varies directly with the nominal long-term interest rate and also depends on the budget constraint and the parameter THETA.

A change in the total nominal value of the portfolio budget is represented in both the money-dividend streams diagram and the money-bonds diagram by a parallel translation of the budget line, with the optimal portfolio points continuing to lie along the same rays from the origin.

A change in the nominal long-term interest rate is represented in the money-dividend streams diagram by a pivoting of the budget line around its MS-intercept which (by Property Two in Section 4) causes the optimal portfolio point to move along a horizontal line. Because the MS-intercept, which represents the total nominal portfolio budget, is unchanged, and because the MS-coordinate of the optimal portfolio point, which represents the nominal value of the money component of the optimal portfolio, is unchanged, therefore, the nominal value of the bond component of the optimal portfolio ($=(100 * DS)/$ ILT) is also unchanged.

In the money-bonds diagram, as the nominal long-term interest rate increases, the budget line and the optimal portfolio point are unchanged, but the value of the utility function increases. In other words, on the money-bonds diagram, as the nominal long-term interest rate increases, the field of portfolio preference curves shrinks uniformly toward the origin.

Note: To highlight the distinctions between the money-dividend streams diagram and the money-bonds diagram, we have assumed in the preceding discussion that the price level was unchanged. However, MS and DS could be replaced in the utility function and in the money-dividend streams diagram by MS/P and DS/P without changing the basic conclusion: that in equilibrium the nominal long-term interest rate is determined by the ratio of MS to DS and by the utility parameter THETA.

Note: If, instead, the indifference curves (portfolio preference curves) were originally defined on the money-bonds diagram rather than the money-dividend streams diagram (that is, originally defined in terms of real money and real perpetual bonds instead of nominal money and the annual nominal dividend stream from perpetual bonds), then the utility of the portfolio preference curves on the money-bonds diagram would be independent of ILT, and the utility of the portfolio preference curves on the money-dividend streams diagram would be a function of ILT. Either way, the essential argument is unchanged, and the value of ILT is the same.

The relations between FA's, money, and perpetual bonds may be summarized as follows:

Stock demand for real FA's = Q * (RST + 100).

Stock demand for real money
= THETA * (Stock demand for real FA's)
= THETA * Q * (RST + 100).

Stock demand for real perpetual bonds
= (1 − THETA) * (Stock demand for real FA's)
= (1 − THETA) * Q * (RST + 100).

Stock supply of real money = MS/P.

Stock supply of real perpetual bonds
= (100 * DS)/(ILT * P).

Stock supply of real FA's
= Stock supply of real money
+ Stock supply of real perpetual bonds
= (MS/P) + ((100 * DS)/(ILT * P)).

In equilibrium:

Stock demand for real money
= Stock supply of real money,

that is:

THETA * (RST + 100) * Q = MS/P.

Stock demand for real perpetual bonds
= Stock supply of real perpetual bonds

that is:

(1 − THETA) * (RST + 100) * Q
= (100 * DS)/(ILT * P).

Stock demand for real FA's
= Stock supply of real FA's

that is:

(RST + 100) * Q
= (MS/P) + ((100 * DS)/(ILT * P)).

In Keynesian theory the additivity of the two components of the stock demand for nominal money means that the nominal money stock supply "supports" either transactions (i.e., real output) or bond purchases but not both. The present model posits the existence of a stock demand function for real FA's which is not additive with respect to Q and RST. With the value of THETA 0.50, the stock demand for real FA's in the present model "supports" both real money and real bonds in equal proportions.

Note: The choice of the Cobb-Douglas form for the utility preference function allows solutions to be found using the constant parameter THETA. The analysis may not be so tidy under alternative functions.

6. Nominal Short-term Interest Rate

This section discusses how the nominal short-term interest rate is derived by the arbitrage relationship between the nominal long-term interest rate at the start of the period and the nominal long-term interest rate at the end of the period.

The nominal long-term interest rate is the interest rate on perpetual bonds. What is the nominal interest rate on money, IST? The value of IST, the nominal short-term interest rate, is determined by the values of ILT and ILTNXT, the values of the nominal long-term interest rate at the start and end of the period. This is because the total return for money and perpetual bonds must be equal in equilibrium. Total return is defined to be the sum of current income and capital gain or loss.

(Note that we neglect reinvestment income. Also note that since money has a constant principal value, the capital gain (or loss) on money equals zero.)

The derivation is as follows:

Current income from a single perp = 1.
Price of perp at start of period = 100/ILT.
Price of perp at end of period = 100/ILTNXT.
Capital gain or loss = 100/ILTNXT − 100/ILT.
Total return from a single perp
$$= 1 + 100/ILTNXT − 100/ILT.$$
Total return per dollar spent on perpetual bonds
$$= ((1 + 100/ILTNXT − 100/ILT)/(100/ILT)) * 100$$
$$= ILT + ((ILT/ILTNXT) − 1) * 100.$$
Total return per dollar spent on one dollar of money = IST.

In equilibrium:

Total return per dollar spent on one dollar of money
    = Total return per dollar spent on perpetual bonds.

Therefore, it follows that:

$$IST = ILT + ((ILT/ILTNXT) - 1) * 100.$$

Note: The present model has no taxes on interest, dividends (i.e., bond coupon payments), or capital gains on perpetual bonds. If such taxes were included, the preceding formula would require adjustment.

Note: If interest on money were zero, then the arbitrage condition among ILT, ILTNXT, and IST would generally not be satisfied, and the model would not always be in equilibrium.

Examples of the Arbitrage Relationship Among ILT, ILTNXT, and IST

	Example 1	Example 2	Example 3
IST	50	110	−45
ILT	25	10	5
ILTNXT	20	5	10
Prep price			
Start of period	4	10	20
End of period	5	20	10
Current income	1	1	1
Capital gain or loss	1	10	−10
Total return	2	11	−9
Rate of return	2/4 = 50%	11/10 = 110%	−9/20 = −45%

If it is expected that the nominal long-term interest rate will be lower at the end of the period than at the start of the period (that is, that holders of perpetual bonds will enjoy capital gains during the period), then the public will attempt to buy bonds and sell money. As a result, the nominal long-term interest rate will fall over the period, and the nominal short-term interest rate at the start of the period must be higher than the nominal long-term interest rate at the start of the period (to equate the total returns on money and perpetual bonds).

If it is expected that the nominal long-term interest rate will be higher at the end of the period than at the start of the period (that is, that holders of perpetual bonds will suffer capital losses during the period), then the public will attempt to sell bonds and buy money. As a result, the nominal long-term interest rate will rise over the period, and the nominal short-term interest rate at the start of the period must be lower than the nominal long-term interest rate at the start of the period (to equate the total returns on money and perpetual bonds).

Note that in the model the nominal short-term interest rate, IST, can be negative if perpetual bonds suffer a large enough capital loss during the period.

What is the timing of the interest and dividend payments on money and perpetual bonds? For the formula above to work, it would appear that both payments should be paid an instant before the end of the period but that the payments should accrue continuously during the period. The nominal interest rate (short-term) on money is a start-of-period value that holds over the entire period.

By regarding money as a short-term asset and perpetual bonds as a long-term asset, the model can be construed to have a rudimentary yield curve, which behaves as follows:

The yield curve would be "flat" (that is, IST = ILT), if and only if ILTNXT = ILT.

The yield curve would be "normal" (that is, IST < ILT), if and only if ILTNXT > ILT.

The yield curve would be "inverted" (that is, IST > ILT), if and only if ILTNXT < ILT.

Note that the model omits risk and assumes that all expectations will be fulfilled.

The conventional belief that an inverted yield curve is an indicator of financial stringency gets support in the sense that it occurs in equilibrium if and only if the nominal long-term interest rate will fall.

Notice that changes in interest rates (real or nominal, long-term or short-term) do not affect the portfolio preferences of the public between money and bonds. These preferences (expressed as indifference curves of a utility function) are determined by the tastes of the public, which are assumed to be fixed. Indeed, the nominal long-term interest rate is derived from the portfolio preferences of the public, and the nominal short-term interest rate is derived by the arbitrage relationship between the nominal long-term interest rates at the start of the period and at the end of the period.

In a sense, if the nominal short-term interest rate failed to respond to these arbitrage possibilities, then the public would get a sure bet on either money or bonds, and either shift the indifference curve field in the direction of either money or bonds or attempt to shift entirely into money or out of money, ignoring its preferences for a portfolio containing both assets.

Such a shift in the indifference curve field might work as follows. If the nominal long-term interest rate were expected to rise, the indifference curves would change so as to cause the public's portfolio preferences to shift away from bonds towards money. If the nominal long-term interest rate were expected to fall, the indifference curves would change so as to cause the public's portfolio preferences to shift away from money towards bonds. These shifts of portfolio preferences do not occur in the present model, since IST adjusts so as to equalize the total returns on money and bonds.

Note: To return briefly to the Keynesian framework, on the IS-LM diagram it is not possible to mix IST and ILT. That is, it is not possible for the IS curve to be a function of IST and the LM curve to be a function of ILT or for the IS curve to be a function of ILT and the LM curve to be a function of IST. The reason is that such mixing leads, over time, to unstable changes in Q, as a consequence of the arbitrage relation between ILT, ILTNXT, and IST.

7. Real Short-term and Long-term Interest Rates

Now that the nominal long-term and short-term interest rates have been derived, what of the corresponding real interest rates? Usually,

$$R = ((100 + I)/(100 + PDOTE)) * 100 - 100,$$

and that procedure can be followed here. The model has a price at the start and end of each period, and in equilibrium the expected and actual rates of inflation (i.e., price change) are equal.

So it is possible to define:

$$RST = ((100 + IST)/(100 + PDOTE)) * 100 - 100.$$

But for the real long-term interest rate the model does not have an actual long-term rate of inflation, much less an expected long-term rate of inflation. The best that can be done is to define

$$RLT = ((100 + ILT)/(100 + PDOTE)) * 100 - 100$$

using the nominal long-term interest rate and the *short-term* expected inflation rate.

3

The 1C Closed-Country Model: Additional Details

1. Possibility of Two Equilibrium Solutions

In the 1C model, for every given stock demand for (and supply of) real financial assets, there are two equilibrium solutions for the model: the RHS (right-hand-side) solution and the LHS (left-hand-side) solution. From a geometric point of view, the RHS and LHS solutions differ in their geometric position in the lower panel of the IS-FA diagram, which contains the stock iso-demand curve field for real FA's, with the RHS solutions lying to the right of the sloping dashed line and the LHS solutions lying to the left of the sloping dashed line.

From an economic point of view, the RHS and LHS solutions differ in the relative effect on the stock demand for real financial assets of a change in real output and a change in the real short-term interest rate.

The algebraic differences between the RHS and LHS solutions are as follows:

A solution for a given period is a RHS solution if and only if:

$$RST < .25 * Q - 100.$$

A solution for a given period is a LHS solution if and only if:

$$RST > .25 * Q - 100.$$

(For completeness, a solution for a given period is called "in the middle" if and only if:

$$RST = .25 * Q - 100.)$$

To see the essential difference between the two solutions, however, both panels of the IS-FA diagram must be compared. It can then be seen that the RHS and LHS solutions differ in the relative slopes of the stock iso-demand curve and the IS-curve. In the RHS solutions, the stock iso-demand curve is flatter than the IS-curve. In the LHS solutions, the IS-curve is flatter than the stock iso-demand curve. (Note: Because there is no maximization occurring on the IS-FA diagram, there is no reason for these slopes to be equal.)

The RHS solution has a higher expected rate of inflation, lower real long-term and short-term interest rates, and higher real saving (and investment) and real output.

The primary difference between the RHS and LHS solutions, and this may be a matter of taste since there are several differences, is the expected rate of inflation. If so, the value of the expected rate of inflation could determine whether an economy has a RHS or LHS solution.

To compare the differences between the RHS and LHS solutions in the 1C model, one can compare the solutions for Period 1 in Simulation 1 (which has a RHS solution) and Simulation 2 (which has a LHS solution), both of which have the same exogenous variables.

Considering Simulation 1 over the entire five-period simulation, the RHS solution appears to produce very high rates of inflation and a higher level of output that cannot be sustained for long in an equilibrium. Considering Simulation 2 over the over the entire five-period simulation, the LHS solution appears, in contrast, to have the more familiar, and more stable, properties normally associated with smoothly functioning economies.

In the 1C model, though not always in the 3C model, the RHS solution appears to be hyperinflationary and not sustainable. The RHS solution shown in Simulation 1 appears to represent virtual expropriation of all real financial assets by means of induced hyperinflation. It would be going too far to assert that all 1C model RHS solutions end this way, but the suspicion that this might be the case accounts for my relative lack of interest in RHS solutions. I grew to believe that only the LHS solutions were sustainable. Lately, especially in the light of the 3C simulations, which do not support this point of view, I am growing more curious and less certain about the RHS solutions. I am also not as certain as I once was that the distinction between LHS and RHS solutions is a useful one, though it may be. For the 1C model, the distinction must be made for some solution routines (see note), which differ for LHS and RHS.

Note: In the 1C model with control variable MSDEL, the LHS and RHS solutions require different arrangements of the equations to produce their solutions. The LHS equation arrangement has Q preceding RLT and uses the convergence of the variable RST; the RHS equation arrangement has RLT preceding Q and uses the convergence of the variable PDOTE.

2. Solution Process

The model consists of a system of simultaneous equations which represent algebraically the relationships among the economic variables in a single time period. Once the values of a small number of independent (so-called exogenous) variables are pre-specified, the equations may be solved for the values of the dependent (so-called endogenous) variables. In the simulation tables the values of exogenous (i.e., pre-specified) variables are shown in italic type.

The flow chart (Figure 20) showing the sequence of computations for a numerical computer model along the lines of the Post Keynesian Macrodynamic framework is typical of several related programs written by the author. This version is for the LHS solution of the 1C model with control variable MSDEL.

The solution process for the Post Keynesian Macrodynamic framework begins with arbitrary values for the stock supply of nominal money, the annual nominal dividend stream from perpetual bonds, and the price level at the start of Period 1 and the change in the nominal money supply during each period of the simulation (for the tables in this book: Periods 1–5). A trial value is selected for the real short-term interest rate at the start of the period.

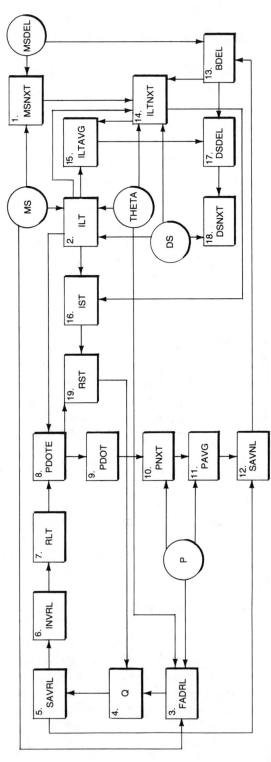

Figure 20 Flow chart for the Post Keynesian Macrodynamic framework (1C model, LHS solution, control variable = MSDEL).

Note: Circles represent exogenous variables. Rectangles represent endogenous variables. Numbers inside rectangles refer to the steps in the solution process.

Step 1: From the stock supply of nominal money at the start of the period and the change in the nominal money supply during the period is found the stock supply of nominal money at the end of the period (the start of the following period).

Step 2: From the stock supply of nominal money at the start of the period, the annual nominal dividend stream from perpetual bonds at the start of the period, and the parameter THETA (from the utility function) is found the nominal long-term interest rate at the start of the period.

Step 3: From the stock supply of nominal money at the start of the period, the price level at the start of the period, and the parameter THETA (from the utility function) is found the stock demand for real FA's at the start of the period.

Step 4: From the stock demand for real FA's at the start of the period and the real short-term interest rate at the start of the period is found real output during the period.

Step 5: From real output during the period is found real saving during the period.

Step 6: Real investment during the period (in the 1C model) equals real saving during the period in equilibrium.

Step 7: From real investment during the period is found the real long-term interest rate at the start of the period.

Step 8: From the real long-term interest rate at the start of the period and the nominal long-term interest rate at the start of the period is found the expected rate of inflation during the period.

Step 9: In equilibrium, the actual rate of inflation during the period equals the expected rate of inflation during the period.

Step 10: From the actual rate of inflation during the period and the price level at the start of the period, is found the price level at the end of the period (the start of the following period).

Step 11: From the price level at the start of the period and the price level at the end of the period is found the average price level during the period.

Step 12: From real saving during the period and the average price level during the period is found nominal saving during the period.

Step 13: From nominal saving during the period and the change in the nominal money supply during the period is found the nominal principal value of perpetual bonds (net) newly issued during the period. (See Section 3 of this chapter.)

Step 14: From the stock supply of nominal money at the end of the period, the annual nominal dividend stream at the start of the period, the nominal long-term interest rate at the start of the period, the nominal principal value of perpetual bonds (net) newly issued during the period, and the utility parameter THETA is found the nominal long-term interest rate at the end of the period (the start of the following period).

Note: The model ensures that the result of Step 14 in the present period will be compatible with the result of Step 2 in the following period.

Step 15: From the nominal long-term interest rate at the start of the period and the nominal long-term interest rate at the end of the period is found the average nominal long-term interest rate during the period.

Step 16: From the nominal long-term interest rate at the start of the period and the nominal long-term interest rate at the end of the period is found the nominal short-term interest rate at the start of the period.

Step 17: From the average nominal long-term interest rate during the period and the nominal principal value of perpetual bonds (net) newly issued during the period is found the change in the annual nominal dividend stream during the period.

Step 18: From the annual nominal dividend stream at the start of the period and the change in the annual nominal dividend stream during the period is found the annual nominal dividend stream at the end of the period (the start of the following period).

Step 19: From the nominal short-term interest rate at the start of the period and the expected rate of inflation during the period is found a (possibly different) value of the real short-term interest rate at the start of the period.

The process is repeated until the value of the real short-term interest rate at the start of the period has the same value at the end of the process as at the start of the process.

By way of a review, the reader should associate the various steps in the solution procedure just outlined with the flow chart and with the IS curve, the stock iso-demand curve field for real FA's, the linking equation, the money-bonds diagram, and the like.

The model can be solved by the Gauss-Seidel method, a computational procedure that solves systems of simultaneous nonlinear equations simply and quickly by means of repeated approximation.

The exact method by which a new trial value is chosen differs from program to program but usually involves viewing the solution process as a function of one variable (sometimes two variables) and employing weighted averages of past values, interpolation procedures, or fixed point formulas.

The convergence criterion was 0.01 meaning that if successive values of the trial variable differed by 0.01 or less from iteration to iteration the approximation was deemed sufficiently close. In any event, calculations were not allowed to run more than 25 iterations (sometimes 35 iterations).

In the computer calculations, all model variables were FOR-TRAN double precision variables. Nevertheless, the solution values may still be inexact not only due to tolerances in the computer programs but also due to inaccuracies in the computer. A pocket calculator offers greater precision.

If a particular simulation fails to converge, it means that the values of the exogenous variables are inconsistent with equilibrium, possibly impossible or unrealistic. Even if an equilibrium solution does exist, it must be checked to make sure that it makes economic sense as well as mathematical sense. The checklists which follow the simulation tables list such conditions.

The model is constructed in such a way that solution values obtained from some endogenous variables may be used as values for some of the exogenous variables in the next period. For example, the endogenous variables MSNXT, DSNXT, and PNXT (created in Steps 1,18, and 10, respectively) become the exogenous variables MS, DS, and P for the following period. In the simulation tables the models have each been solved period by period, for a total of five periods, by this process of chaining the one-period solutions together, period to period. Exogenous variables shown as start-of-period variables for

Periods 2–6 are, in the actual computations, end-of-period variables for Periods 1–5.

The zeros in Period 6 of the simulation tables represent values not calculated by the model. In the computer programs, the matrices which ultimately become the simulation tables are initially filled with zeros. As the values of the variables are computed, the zeros are replaced by the computed values. The zeros remaining in Period 6 represent variables whose values were not defined at the end of Period 5 (the last period computed).

For each simulation of five periods, the exogenous variables required are the initial values of MS, DS, and P at the start of the first period and the values of the control variable MSDEL during each of the five periods. Note: Calling MSDEL a control variable is meant to indicate merely that it is an exogenous variable whose value cannot be obtained from the values of endogenous variables in the previous period. In contrast to the initial variables, which are exogenous variables whose values can be obtained in this way.

Once the values are given for the initial variables at the start of the first period, the entire path of the simulation depends only on the values of the control variable.

By varying MSDEL, the change in the nominal money supply during the period, the authorities control the course of the economy, including BDEL, the nominal principal value of perpetual bonds (net) newly issued during the period. The more money issued during the period, the fewer bonds issued.

Note: In effect the model assumes that the authorities can control MSDEL by facilitating or impeding the saving-investment process in addition to the means of central bank money-bond operations, central bank foreign exchange operations, and government operations to finance the budget deficit.

To see the effect of a change in MSDEL on the 1C LHS solution, one can compare the solutions for Period 1 in Simulations 2 and 3, whose exogenous variables differ only in their value for MSDEL.

It is sometimes claimed that higher monetary growth in the short run reduces real interest rates. However, in the LHS solution to the 1C model, as seen by comparing Period 1 in

Simulations 2 and 3, a higher rate of monetary growth results in higher real short-term and long-term interest rates, a higher nominal short-term interest rate, lower real investment and real output, lower inflation, and lower nominal long-term interest rates at the end of the period (i.e., the start of the next period). Of course, these two examples are only particular instances, not general cases. And it must be continually emphasized that the present model is an equilibrium model.

In choosing the values of the control variable MSDEL, no optimization has been undertaken, in part because of the lack of an obviously suitable objective function and in part because of the complexity of the task if one had been selected.

The model also can be solved in a backward direction (using MSNXT, DSNXT, PNXT, and MSDEL as exogenous variables), which suggests that dynamic programming techniques could be used, providing a criterion function could be established. (Such a dynamic programming problem would be continuous-state, discrete-time problem, which is more complex than a discrete-state, discrete-time problem.)

The possibility of being able to solve in both a forward and backward direction also suggests that it might be possible to define a more complex (though less intuitive) long-term expected (and actual) rate of price change.

Note: The present form of the model ignores the extent to which payments of interest on money and dividends on perpetual bonds would (or might) tend to increase the stock supply of nominal money. This omission simplifies the model without, I believe, significantly changing its nature.

3. Money-Bond Operations

The reason there has been no discussion of central bank money-bond operations in the domestic currency is that such operations have no effect on the model solution. That is, the disposition of the increase in the nominal money supply between investment (capital formation) and money-bond operations is immaterial. In the 1C model, once the values of the exogenous initial variables (MS, DS, and P) are given, the value of the exogenous control variable (MSDEL) completely determines the solution, including the net new issue of perpetual bonds during the period, the average price level during the period, real investment, and real and nominal saving during the period.

What happens with money-bond operations is that a specified increase in open market sales of money—or, equivalently, open market purchases of perpetual bonds—causes an equal reduction in the sales of new money for capital formation purposes and an equal increase in the sales of new perpetual bonds for capital formation purposes.

Similarly, a specified decrease in open market sales of money—or, equivalently, open market purchases of perpetual bonds—causes an equal increase in the sales of new money for capital formation purposes and an equal decrease in the sales of new perpetual bonds for capital formation purposes.

For example, consider the following cases:

Case 1: The central bank sells $10 of money to the public and buys $10 of bonds from the public, and the investors in the private sector sell $10 of new money and $15 of new bonds to the savers in the private sector (for purposes of capital formation). The total increase in money held by the public is $20 and in bonds held by the public is $5. The total nominal saving (and investment) of the public is $25.

Case 2: The central bank sells $6 of money to the public and buys $6 of bonds from the public, and the investors in the private sector sell $14 of new money and $11 of new bonds to the savers in the private sector (for purposes of capital formation). Once again the total increase in money held by the public is $20 and in bonds held by the public is $5. And again the total nominal saving (and investment) of the public is $25.

Comment: In both cases the model sees the total increase in money held by the public ($20) as the only independent variable (except, of course, for the initial variables of MS, DS, and P), from which it computes the entire solution, including the values of total increase in bonds of $5 and the total nominal saving (and investment) of $25.

The irrelevance of money-bond operations to the model solutions also holds for the 3C floating and fixed exchange rate models and for the 1C(F) model.

Note: The numbers used in the preceding example are chosen solely for illustrative purposes. They would not necessarily be generated by the model.

Note: Because the model is in equilibrium at all times, the money-bond open market operations must be gradual (or smooth).

4. Policy Considerations

The variable MSDEL can be used to control many alternative variables, including MSNXT, IST, and ILTNXT. Therefore, there is no conflict in this model between controlling money growth, nominal short-term interest rates, and nominal long-term interest rates. Any chosen path of MSDEL will determine all three. However, which path of MSDEL should be chosen? One path may produce the desired path of MSNXT, a second path may produce the desired path of IST, and a third path may produce the desired path for ILTNXT. If the paths differ, the goals conflict.

The following questions are heard often:

Is it true that monetary policy primarily affects inflation and that fiscal policy primarily affects real output?

Should fiscal policy be loose to boost growth?

Should monetary policy be tight to stop inflation?

Is the present policy mix a good one?

What is the proper definition of monetary policy? Of fiscal policy? Of foreign exchange policy?

These questions usually mean different things to different people, because terms like monetary policy, fiscal policy, and foreign exchange policy do not always refer clearly to a particular exogenous variable.

In the real world, as distinct from the model, policy makers directly control certain variables called policy instruments (which are tools or levers of policy) in order to effect a change in the value of variables called policy targets (which are the goals or objects of policy). Each policy instrument variable, may be employed to ultimately influence one of many alternative policy target variables. Thus, changes in MSDEL may be used to control, alternatively, MSDEL, MSNXT, ILTNXT, IST, RST, RLT, INVRL, Q, or PDOTE. The first four of these variables have two equilibrium solutions consistent with the particular values of the target variables, a LHS solution and a RHS solution. The last five variables have only a single equilibrium solution consistent with the particular values of the target variables, which may contain periods of both LHS and RHS solutions within the course of a single multiperiod simulation. (Each period has a solution which is either LHS or RHS, unless it is exactly midway between them.) Thus, two values of Q are consistent with a single value of MSDEL, MSNXT, ILTNXT or IST, but only one value of Q is consistent with a single value of RST, RLT, INVRL, Q, or PDOTE. Many other targets are possible. However, for some the calculations might be much more complex.

In the model's computer programs and simulations the process is reversed, with the policy target being an exogenous control variable and the policy instrument, if different, being an endogenous variable. This is why the policy targets appear as exogenous control variables in Program 3 and Simulation 4 (with ILTNXT), Program 4 and Simulation 5 (with Q), and Program 6 and Simulations 7–9 (with KNXT and HNXT). (The programs are described in Appendix 1.)

4

The 1C Closed-Country Model: Simulation Results

1. 1C Simulation Notes

Note that the condition that IST be positive is in the checklists not for mathematical or economic reasons, but merely because negative nominal short-term interest rates are rarely, if ever, found in the real world. In Simulation 1, Period 4, and in Simulation 5, Periods 3, 4, and 5, IST is negative, because holders of perpetual bonds had capital losses large enough to cause negative total returns. To equalize the total returns on money and perpetual bonds, the nominal short-term interest rate on money had to be negative.

A simulation which attempted to peg IST = 38 for Periods 1–5 failed to converge for Period 1 and is not included in the book. (No value of MSDEL existed that could produce IST = 38 for Period 1 in a way that was consistent with equilibrium.)

The program proceeded with the calculations, however, for Periods 2–5, which converged. Thus, if the model had been started at the values for Period 2, (which were MS = 1994.84893, DS = 808.53133, P = 0.18501) it would have been possible to peg IST = 38 for Periods 2–5. The interesting aspect of this simulation was that ILTNXT was not stabilized. ILT was 40.53096 in Period 2 and increased monotonically thereafter. This is a consequence of the arbitrage relationship between nominal long-term interest rates and nominal short-term interest rates. Attempts to peg nominal short-term interest rates below nominal long-term interest rates will only produce rising nominal long-term interest rates in the model. Trying to peg ILTNXT = 38 for Periods 1–5 (i.e., ILT for Periods 2–6) shown in Simulation 4 will also stabilize IST for Periods 2–5.

Inasmuch as these last points may have some relevance to the conduct of monetary policy, it may be worthwhile to restate them in more general terms. Fixing IST for several periods at a level below ILT in the first period causes ILT to rise monotonically in subsequent periods, because a value of IST below ILT implies a value of ILTNXT above ILT, from the arbitrage relation. Therefore, the following period ILT (the former ILTNXT) is even more above IST, causing the process to accelerate.

On the other hand, fixing ILTNXT (instead of IST) for several periods at a level below ILT in the first period causes IST and ILT at the start of the second period to equal the pegged value.

2. 1C Variables

List of Variable Names for 1C Model
Shown in Simulations 1–5

MS = nominal money supply, start of period.

MSDEL = change in nominal money supply during period.

DS = annual nominal dividend stream from perpetual bonds, start of period.

RLT = real long-term interest rate, start of period.

INVRL = real investment during period.

Q = real output during period.

FADRL = stock demand for real financial assets, start of period.

P = price level, start of period.

ILT = nominal long-term interest rate, start of period.

PDOTE = expected rate of price change during period.

PAVG = price level, average over period.

SAVNL = nominal saving during period.

BDEL = nominal principal value of perpetual bonds (net) newly issued during period.

ILTAVG = nominal long-term interest rate, average over period.

DSDEL = change in annual nominal dividend stream from perpetual bonds during period.

IST = nominal short-term interest rate, start of period.

RST = real short-term interest rate, start of period.

List of Variable Names for 1C Model
Not Shown in Simulations 1–5

MSNXT = nominal money supply, end of period.

SAVRL = real saving during period.

PNXT = price level, end of period.

INVNL = nominal investment during period.

ILTNXT = nominal long-term interest rate, end of period.

DSNXT = annual nominal dividend stream from perpetual bonds, end of period.

PDOT = actual rate of price change realized during period.

3. Tables for 1C Simulations 1–5

This section contains tables for Simulations 1–5, numerical examples of the 1C model. In the simulation tables the values in italics are exogenous.

Simulation 1, 1C MSDEL RHS.

Scenario: Hyperinflationary financial collapse. Unsustainable. Only pure RHS simulation.

Variable	Period 1	Period 2	Period 3	Period 4	Period 5	Period 6
MS	2010.00000	2040.00000	2075.00000	2115.00000	2160.00000	2210.00000
MSDEL	30.00000	35.00000	40.00000	45.00000	50.00000	0.00000
DS	800.00000	790.19122	783.58941	825.35388	6136.37241	82868267907.39181
RLT	-12.02702	-60.81263	-90.06444	-98.19772	-99.98787	0.00000
INVRL	39.81081	59.32505	71.02577	74.27908	74.99514	0.00000
Q	448.10823	643.25072	760.25800	792.79113	799.95173	0.00000
FADRL	40200.01438	25674.34457	7376.45766	542.24917	7.17920	0.00023
P	0.10000	0.15891	0.56260	7.80084	601.73861	19048191.84587
ILT	39.80100	38.73486	37.76335	39.02382	284.09132	3749695380.42497
PDOTE	58.90622	254.03361	1286.57244	7613.76290	3165425.96396	0.00000
PAVG	0.12606	0.29901	2.09494	68.51327	107060.88193	0.00000
SAVNL	5.01859	17.73857	148.79448	5089.10274	8029046.27709	0.00000
BDEL	-24.98141	-17.26143	108.79448	5044.10274	8028996.27709	0.00000
ILTAVG	39.26431	38.24602	38.38841	105.29164	1032112.34519	0.00000
DSDEL	-9.80878	-6.60181	41.76447	5311.01853	82868261771.01941	0.00000
IST	42.55338	41.30751	34.53332	-47.23981	184.09132	0.00000
RST	-10.28950	-60.08657	-90.29743	-99.31603	-99.99103	0.00000

Simulation 2, 1C MSDEL LHS.

Scenario: A maintainable equilibrium.
Note: The exogenous variables are the same for Simulations 1 and 2.

Variable	Period 1	Period 2	Period 3	Period 4	Period 5	Period 6
MS	*2010.00000*	2040.00000	2075.00000	2115.00000	2160.00000	2210.00000
MSDEL	*30.00000*	35.00000	*40.00000*	*45.00000*	*50.00000*	0.00000
DS	*800.00000*	789.54336	777.01266	763.15112	748.10263	732.02804
RLT	12.27472	44.74210	39.21309	35.93138	33.80346	0.00000
INVRL	30.09011	17.10316	19.31476	20.62745	21.47862	0.00000
Q	350.90124	221.03167	243.14773	256.27459	264.78625	0.00000
FADRL	40200.01438	32766.65039	34779.92797	35906.05384	36629.20993	37245.81250
P	*0.10000*	0.12452	0.11932	0.11781	0.11794	0.11867
ILT	39.80100	38.70311	37.44639	36.08280	34.63438	33.12344
PDOTE	24.51689	−4.17225	−1.26906	0.11139	0.62100	0.00000
PAVG	0.11159	0.12189	0.11856	0.11787	0.11830	0.00000
SAVNL	3.35767	2.08473	2.29000	2.43142	2.54101	0.00000
BDEL	−26.64233	−32.91527	−37.71000	−42.56858	−47.45899	0.00000
ILTAVG	39.24821	38.06956	36.75827	35.35117	33.87049	0.00000
DSDEL	−10.45664	−12.53070	−13.86154	−15.04849	−16.07459	0.00000
IST	42.63769	42.05914	41.22547	40.26481	39.19592	0.00000
RST	14.56219	48.24414	43.04031	40.10774	38.33502	0.00000

Simulation 3, 1C MSDEL LHS.

Scenario: Same as Simulation 2 with 10 percent increase in nominal money growth.

Variable	Period 1	Period 2	Period 3	Period 4	Period 5	Period 6
MS	2010.00000	2043.00000	2081.50000	2125.50000	2175.00000	2230.00000
MSDEL	33.00000	38.50000	44.00000	49.50000	55.00000	0.00000
DS	800.00000	788.36451	774.57104	759.36859	742.93301	725.45541
RLT	13.07600	44.18732	38.72391	35.41406	33.17330	0.00000
INVRL	29.76960	17.32507	19.51044	20.83438	21.73068	0.00000
Q	347.69614	223.25079	245.10445	258.34387	267.30691	0.00000
FADRL	40200.01438	33049.02752	35032.11850	36166.77917	36923.83581	37579.71749
P	0.10000	0.12363	0.11883	0.11754	0.11781	0.11868
ILT	39.80100	38.58857	37.21216	35.72659	34.15784	32.53163
PDOTE	23.63454	-3.88297	-1.08976	0.23080	0.73929	0.00000
PAVG	0.11119	0.12121	0.11818	0.11767	0.11824	0.00000
SAVNL	3.31011	2.09998	2.30583	2.45167	2.56954	0.00000
BDEL	-29.68989	-36.40002	-41.69417	-47.04833	-52.43046	0.00000
ILTAVG	39.19009	37.89411	36.46181	34.93341	33.33482	0.00000
DSDEL	-11.63549	-13.79347	-15.20245	-16.43558	-17.47760	0.00000
IST	42.94292	42.28740	41.37032	40.31923	39.15669	0.00000
RST	15.61824	48.03543	42.92731	39.99472	38.13274	0.00000

Simulation 4, 1C ILTNXT LHS.

Scenario: Pegging the nominal long-term interest rate on perpetual bonds.

Variable	Period 1	Period 2	Period 3	Period 4	Period 5	Period 6
MS	*2010.00000*	2058.64743	2059.84736	2061.04179	2062.23585	2063.43041
MSDEL	48.64743	1.19993	1.19443	1.19406	1.19456	0.00000
DS	*800.00000*	782.28602	782.74200	783.19588	783.64962	784.10355
RLT	16.71854	37.50026	37.84705	37.90689	37.91770	0.00000
INVRL	28.31259	19.99990	19.86118	19.83724	19.83292	0.00000
Q	333.12598	249.99905	248.61189	248.37253	248.32928	0.00000
FADRL	40200.01438	34374.91989	34270.40172	34252.26908	34248.98973	34248.39246
P	*0.10000*	0.11978	0.12021	0.12034	0.12043	0.12050
ILT	39.80100	*38.00000*	*38.00000*	*38.00000*	*38.00000*	*38.00000*
PDOTE	19.77617	0.36345	0.11096	0.06752	0.05967	0.00000
PAVG	0.10944	0.11999	0.12028	0.12039	0.12046	0.00000
SAVNL	3.09859	2.39986	2.38887	2.38812	2.38911	0.00000
BDEL	−45.54884	1.19993	1.19443	1.19406	1.19456	0.00000
ILTAVG	38.89007	38.00000	38.00000	38.00000	38.00000	0.00000
DSDEL	−17.71398	0.45597	0.45388	0.45374	0.45393	0.00000
IST	44.54046	38.00000	38.00000	38.00000	38.00000	0.00000
RST	20.67511	37.50020	37.84699	37.90683	37.91765	0.00000

Simulation 5, 1C Q.

Scenario: Pegging real output. Solved recursively, not by iteration.
Note: This simulation has a different initial value of DS from other 1C and 1C(F) simulations.
Note: Period 1 has a LHS solution; Periods 2–5 have RHS solutions.

Variable	Period 1	Period 2	Period 3	Period 4	Period 5	Period 6
MS	*2010.00000*	2017.00502	1987.03680	1903.42159	1745.36765	1491.93406
MSDEL	7.00502	−29.96822	−83.61520	−158.05395	−253.43358	0.00000
DS	*80.00000*	79.86360	81.21848	84.95473	92.85253	0.00000
RLT	0.00004	0.00004	0.00004	0.00004	0.00004	0.00000
INVRL	34.99999	34.99999	34.99999	34.99999	34.99999	0.00000
Q	*400.00000*	400.00000	400.00000	400.00000	400.00000	0.00000
FADRL	40200.01438	38796.00955	36763.92764	33833.96596	29698.97094	24104.25197
P	*0.10000*	0.10398	0.10810	0.11252	0.11754	0.12379
ILT	3.98010	3.95951	4.08742	4.46326	5.31994	7.29985
PDOTE	3.98006	3.95948	4.08738	4.46323	5.31990	0.00000
PAVG	0.10197	0.10602	0.11028	0.11500	0.12062	0.00000
SAVNL	3.56897	3.71065	3.85994	4.02496	4.22181	0.00000
BDEL	−3.43606	33.67887	87.47515	162.07891	257.65539	0.00000
ILTAVG	3.96979	4.02296	4.27121	4.87281	6.23176	0.00000
DSDEL	−0.13640	1.35489	3.73625	7.89780	16.05646	0.00000
IST	4.50000	0.83032	−4.33348	−11.63987	−21.80268	0.00000
RST	0.50004	−3.00998	−8.09018	−15.41509	−25.75257	0.00000

4. 1C Checklist

This section lists conditions for the solutions of the 1C model that are necessary for equilibrium and/or desirable for realism.

The checklist for the 1C model (with no fiscal policy) follows:

MS > 0.
DS > 0.
ILT > 0.
P > 0.
MSNXT > 0.
DSNXT > 0.
ILTNXT > 0.
PNXT > 0.
INVRL > 0.
SAVRL > 0.
FADRL > 0.
Q > 0.
PAVG > 0.
ILTAVG > 0.
IST > 0.
ILT = ((DS * THETA)/(MS * (1 − THETA))) * 100.
MSNXT = MSDEL + MS.
FADRL = MS/(P * THETA).
Q = FADRL/(RST + 100).
SAVRL = − 5 + .1 * Q.
INVRL = SAVRL.
INVRL = 35 − .4 * RLT.
PDOTE = ((100 + ILT)/(100 + RLT)) * 100 − 100.
PDOT = PDOTE.
PNXT = P * (1 + (PDOT/100)).
PAVG = DSQRT(P * PNXT).
SAVNL = SAVRL * PAVG.
BDEL = SAVNL − MSDEL.
ILTAVG = DSQRT(ILT * ILTNXT).
DSDEL = (ILTAVG/100) * BDEL.
DSNXT = DS + DSDEL.
IST = ILT + ((ILT/ILTNXT) − 1) * 100.
RST = ((100 + IST)/(100 + PDOTE)) * 100 − 100.

5. 1C Questions and Issues

This section lists some questions about the macroeconomy that can be addressed by the 1C model.

What is the effect of an increase in MSDEL on Q? P? PDOTE? ILTNXT? IST? RLT? RST? Under the LHS and RHS solutions?

Does pegging IST or ILTNXT too high or too low cause excessive monetary growth or inflation? Or recession? Are any of the interest rate variables (ILT, IST, RLT, RST) high because of expectations of inflation, expectations of future increases in real output, or for some other reasons, such as the relative supplies of money and perpetual bonds?

Are high interest rates (ILT, IST, RLT, RST) causing recession?

Is the recession causing high interest rates (ILT, IST, RLT, RST)?

How is the recession affecting the private sector's need for credit? Its supply of saving?

Will an economic upturn raise or lower nominal or real interest rates?

What are the effects of changing the values of the initial exogenous variables?

What are the effects of changing the values of the control exogenous variable(s)?

What are the effects of changing the values of any or all of the exogenous variables?

How do the LHS and RHS solutions differ, if both exist?
What are the effects of changing the sequences of LHS and/or RHS solutions in those cases where a deliberate choice must be made whether to solve for a LHS solution or a RHS solution?

What is the effect of a change in portfolio preferences between real money and real perpetual bonds (i.e., in the parameter THETA)?

What is the effect of a change in the real FA stock demand function?

What is the effect of a change in the saving rate? (Note: Although the saving rate is not an explicit variable in the model, it appears implicitly in the equation which relates real saving to real output.)

If the model contained an explicit saving rate, should that rate be a function of RST? Of RLT? Either choice would make the model somewhat classical in tone.

5

The 3C International Model: Theoretical Background

The arbitrage relationship among ILT, ILTNXT, and IST that existed in the 1C world carries over into the 3C world. The first section introduces some additional arbitrage relationships that exist only in the 3C world. The following sections introduce the 3C model. The 3C model variables are listed and defined in Section 2 of Chapter 6.

1. Arbitrage Conditions

In addition to the parity between the nominal short-term interest rate and the nominal long-term interest rate the following arbitrage relationships hold in equilibrium.

1. Purchasing power parity between the price of goods in domestic and foreign currencies and the exchange rate between the two currencies.
   K = PA/PB,
   H = PA/PC.
   Note: There are no tariffs in the model.
2. Inflation parity between actual inflation rates in domestic and foreign currencies and the actual change in the exchange rate between the two currencies.
   KDOT = ((100 + PDOTA)/(100 + PDOTB)) * 100 − 100,
   HDOT = ((100 + PDOTA)/(100 + PDOTC)) * 100 − 100.

3. Interest rate parity between nominal short-term interest rates in domestic and foreign currencies and the expected change in the exchange rate between the two currencies.
KDOTE = ((100 + ISTA)/(100 + ISTB)) * 100 - 100,
HDOTE = ((100 + ISTA)/(100 + ISTC)) * 100 - 100.

Under fixed exchange rates, in equilibrium, the actual and expected rates of change in all exchange rates are zero. That is,

$$KDOT = KDOTE = HDOT = HDOTE = 0.$$

This implies that the nominal short-term interest rates are equal in all currencies and that the actual (and expected) inflation rates are equal in all currencies. That is:

$$ISTA = ISTB = ISTC,$$

and

$$PDOTA = PDOTEA = PDOTB = PDOTEB$$
$$= PDOTC = PDOTEC.$$

The real short-term interest rate is equal in all currencies in equilibrium. This result follows from the equations given in paragraphs 2 and 3 above as well as from the equality in equilibrium of the actual and expected inflation rates in each currency and the actual and expected rates of change in the exchange rates between any two currencies.
That is:

$$PDOTA = PDOTEA,$$
$$PDOTB = PDOTEB,$$
$$PDOTC = PDOTEC,$$
$$KDOT = KDOTE,$$
and $$HDOT = HDOTE.$$

A proof that RST is the same in all currencies in equilibrium is the following.
From

$$KDOT = KDOTE$$

and

$$KDOT = ((100 + PDOTA)/(100 + PDOTB)) * 100 - 100$$

and

$$KDOTE = ((100 + ISTA)/(100 + ISTB)) * 100 - 100,$$

it follows that

$$(100 + PDOTA)/(100 + ISTA)$$
$$= (100 + PDOTB)/(100 + ISTB).$$

And from

$$HDOT = HDOTE$$

and

$$HDOT = ((100 + PDOTA)/(100 + PDOTC)) * 100 - 100$$

and

$$HDOTE = ((100 + ISTA)/(100 + ISTC)) * 100 - 100,$$

it follows that

$$(100 + PDOTA)/(100 + ISTA)$$
$$= (100 + PDOTC)/(100 + ISTC).$$

From these two results and

$$PDOTA = PDOTEA$$

and

$$PDOTB = PDOTEB$$

and

$$PDOTC = PDOTEC,$$

it follows that

$$(100 + PDOTEA)/(100 + ISTA)$$
$$= (100 + PDOTEB)/(100 + ISTB)$$

and

$$(100 + PDOTEA)/(100 + ISTA)$$
$$= (100 + PDOTEC)/(100 + ISTC).$$

From these last two results and

$$RSTA = ((100 + ISTA)/(100 + PDOTEA)) * 100 - 100$$

and

$$RSTB = ((100 + ISTB)/(100 + PDOTEB)) * 100 - 100$$

and

$$RSTC = ((100 + ISTC)/(100 + PDOTEC)) * 100 - 100,$$

it follows that

$$RSTA = RSTB$$

and

$$RSTA = RSTC,$$

which was asserted.

Therefore, the final A, B, and C can be dropped from RSTA, RSTB, and RSTC, respectively, and the three variables can be interchangeably referred to as RST.

2. 3C International Extension

This section and the ones that follow it introduce the 3C model. The international model is a three-country, three-currency model closely based on the one-country, one-currency closed economy model. The decision to have three countries was made because a model with only two countries may obscure some of the complexities of international economic interactions whereas a model with four or more countries might get bogged down in unnecessary details.

The use of a three-country model allows the study of such phenomena as competition between exporters of two countries in a third-country market. Note the absence from the model of trade-weighted exchange rates, which fail to capture many interrelationships. If the two exporting countries mentioned above did not trade with each other, the degree of their economic interconnection might be obscured if trade-weighted exchange rates were used.

In any case, the reader can generalize the two- or four- (or more) country cases from the three country example. The three countries and currencies are called A, B, and C. Whether the country or currency is being referred to can be seen from the context.

The variables in the 3C model are listed and defined in Section 2 of Chapter 6. The following account will serve as a quick overview. Some variables refer to country, others to currency. Thus, QA, QB, and QC represent real output of the three countries. INVRLA, INVRLB, and INVRLC represent real investment of the three countries. SUNA, SUNB, and SUNC represent real saving of the three countries. FUNA, FUNB, and FUNC represent the stock demands for real FA's by country. These last variables must be distinguished from FURA, FURB, and FURC, which represent the stock demands for real FA's by currency.

Each currency has a price level (PA, PB, PC), an actual inflation rate (PDOTA, PDOTB, PDOTC), an expected inflation rate (PDOTEA, PDOTEB, PDOTEC), a nominal long-term interest rate (ILTA, ILTB, ILTC), a nominal short-term interest rate (ISTA, ISTB, ISTC), a real long-term interest rate (RLTA, RLTB, RLTC), and a real short-term interest rate (RSTA, RSTB, and RSTC, which are all equal in equilibrum and denoted by RST).

MSA, MSB, and MSC represent the global nominal money supplies in the three currencies, and DSA, DSB, and DSC represent the global nominal annual dividend streams from perpetual bonds in the three currencies. The next variable differs between the 3C models with floating and fixed exchange rates. In the 3C model with floating exchange rates, MSDELA, MSDELB, and MSDELC represent the (net) changes during the period in the global nominal money supply in each currency. In the 3C model with fixed exchange rates, MLTOTA, MLTOTB, and MLTOTC represent the (net) changes during the period in the global nominal money supply in each currency. Each of these (net) changes is the sum of two components, MLFXA and MLNFXA, MLFXB and MLNFXB, and MLFXC and MLNFXC, representing the portion of the (net) changes due to foreign exchange operations and other causes, respectively.

DSDELA, DSDELB, and DSDELC represent the (net) changes during the period in the global nominal annual dividend streams from perpetual bonds in the three currencies. BDELA,

BDELB, and BDELC represent the (net) new bond issues during the period in the three currencies given in terms of the principal value of bonds (net) newly issued during the period.

For each currency, there is a global market for money and a global market for bonds. In these markets the supply is the total outstanding stock supply of money or bonds in the currency held by the public in the three countries, and the demand is the sum of the stock demands by the public in the three countries for money or bonds in the currency.

The following equations summarize some of the relationships. Other relationships are presented in Section 4.

Stock demand for real FA's by Country A
= Stock demand by Country A for real FA's in Currency A
+ Stock demand by Country A for real FA's in Currency B
+ Stock demand by Country A for real FA's in Currency C.

Stock demand for real FA's by Country B
= Stock demand by Country B for real FA's in Currency A
+ Stock demand by Country B for real FA's in Currency B
+ Stock demand by Country B for real FA's in Currency C.

Stock demand for real FA's by Country C
= Stock demand by Country C for real FA's in Currency A
+ Stock demand by Country C for real FA's in Currency B
+ Stock demand by Country C for real FA's in Currency C.

Real saving by Country A
    = Real saving by Country A in Currency A
    + Real saving by Country A in Currency B
    + Real saving by Country A in Currency C.

Real saving by Country B
    = Real saving by Country B in Currency A
    + Real saving by Country B in Currency B
    + Real saving by Country B in Currency C.

Real saving by Country C
    = Real saving by Country C in Currency A
    + Real saving by Country C in Currency B
    + Real saving by Country C in Currency C.

Global stock supply of (= demand for) real FA's in Currency A
= Stock supply of (= demand for) real FA's
in Currency A by Country A
+ Stock supply of (= demand for) real FA's
in Currency A by Country B
+ Stock supply of (= demand for) real FA's
in Currency A by Country C.

Global stock supply of (= demand for) real FA's in Currency B
= Stock supply of (= demand for) real FA's
in Currency B by Country A
+ Stock supply of (= demand for) real FA's
in Currency B by Country B
+ Stock supply of (= demand for) real FA's
in Currency B by Country C.

Global stock supply of (= demand for) real FA's in Currency C
= Stock supply of (= demand for) real FA's
in Currency C by Country A
+ Stock supply of (= demand for) real FA's
in Currency C by Country B
+ Stock supply of (= demand for) real FA's
in Currency C by Country C.

The next section will describe how the model constructs the individual terms on the right-hand side of these equations from the terms on the left-hand side.

3. The Currency Preference Matrix and its Inverse

This section introduces the currency preference matrix and its inverse. These two matrices play a central role in the following processes:

1. The translation of real saving by country into real saving by currency.
2. The translation of the stock demand for real FA's by country into the stock demand for real FA's by currency.

3. The translation of the stock supply of (= demand for) real FA's by currency into the stock supply of (= demand for) real FA's by country.

The 3C model can also be seen as a generalization of the 1C model in terms of the IS-FA diagram, the linking equation, and the money-bonds diagram. Of the variables that go (directly or indirectly) into the IS-FA diagram, RLT and RST are currency variables, and INVRL, SAVRL, Q, and FADRL are country variables. Of the variables that go into the linking equation, SAVRL, PAVG, MSDEL, and BDEL are all currency variables. And of the variables that go into the money-bonds diagram, MS, P, DS, ILT, and, implicitly, FADRL are all currency variables.

To solve the 3C model it must be possible to go from FADRL as a country variable to FADRL as a currency variable (and *vice versa*), and from SAVRL as a country variable to SAVRL as a currency variable (though not, in the present model, *vice versa*).

The extension of the 1C model to the 3C model is not entirely straightforward, because of the danger of confusing real FA demands (= supplies) and real saving by country with real FA demands (= supplies) and real saving by currency, respectively.

The three countries are assumed to have portfolio preferences among the three currencies defined by the currency preference matrix below:

One unit of stock demand for real FA's by country or one unit of real saving by country . . .

. . . becomes the number of units of stock demand for real FA's by currency or units of real saving by currency indicated below.

Country	Currency		
	A	B	C
A	.8	.1	.1
B	.4	.4	.2
C	.1	.1	.8

Notice that the row elements add up to one real unit.

Because no two countries have identical preferences, it is possible to go backwards also using the currency preference inverse matrix below:

One unit of stock supply of   . . . becomes the number of
   (= demand for) real FA's   units of stock supply of
   by currency . . .   (= demand for) real FA's
                                       by country indicated be-
                                       low.

Currency	**Country**		
	A	**B**	**C**
A	10/7	− 1/3	− 2/21
B	− 10/7	3	− 4/7
C	0	− 1/3	4/3

Notice that once again the row elements add up to one real unit.

The currency preference matrix distributes the stock demand for real FA's by country over the three currencies. The currency preference matrix shows that in the 3C model, Country A prefers to keep 80 percent of its FA's in Currency A, 10 percent in Currency B, and 10 percent in Currency C; whereas Country B prefers to keep 40 percent of its FA's in Currency A, 40 percent in Currency B, and 20 percent in Currency C; and Country C prefers to keep 10 percent of its FA's in Currency A, 10 percent in Currency B, and 80 percent in Currency C. The only constraint on the currency preference matrix is that no two countries can have the same preferences. In such a situation the model could not tell the two countries apart. (Technically, it would not be possible to compute the currency preference inverse matrix.)

The preferences embodied in currency preference matrix (and its inverse) tell nothing about the distribution, for any combination of country and currency, of preferences between money and bonds. What proportion of the 40 percent of its

FA's that Country B prefers to keep in Currency A does Country B prefer to keep in money and what proportion in bonds? Is it 10 percent money and 90 percent bonds for Country B's holdings of FA's in Currency A, or 50-50, or 70-30? This money-bond mix is determined by the parameter THETA in the country's money-bonds portfolio preference utility function for the particular currency. In the present 3C model, this utility function is the same for each combination of country and currency, and the parameter THETA is also the same (i.e., namely, 0.50). A more general approach is discussed in Appendix 4.

In the 3C model the same set of portfolio preferences is used to translate both the stock demand for real FA's and real saving from country to currency. Although the preferences for currencies by each country need not be the same for both the stock demand for real FA's and real saving, it seems reasonable that they might be, since saving is the acquisition of newly issued FA's and the stock demand for real FA's is the total portfolio holding. It seems plausible in equilibrium that a holder would acquire assets in each period in the same proportion in which they would ultimately be held. (This assumption also simplifies the model.) However, the reader will notice that the force of such logic is hardly compelling. In the 1C and 3C models the parameter THETA measures the proportion of real money in the total portfolio of real money plus real bonds; nevertheless, the acquisition of (net) new nominal money in each period is a policy variable under the control of the central bank and is not, in either model, a fixed proportion THETA of nominal saving for the period.

A value of MSDEL which causes the ratio of the change in the nominal money supply during the period to the change in the annual nominal dividend stream from perpetual bonds during the period (i.e., the ratio MSDEL/DSDEL) to be the same as the ratio of the stock supply of real money to the stock supply of real perpetual bonds at the start of the period (i.e., THETA/(1 − THETA)) represents a policy of setting ILTNXT equal to ILT, that is, of keeping the nominal long-term interest rate unchanged. For an example of this situation, see Simulation 4.

4. Equilibrium Equations

This section provides a less compressed version of the equations which the 3C model satisfies in dynamic equilibrium.

In terms of the connection between the supply of and demand for real and nominal money and bonds, the model assumes that the stock demand for real FA's by country is a positive function of both real output by country and the real short-term interest rate. These stock demands for real FA's by country are translated into stock demands for real FA's by currency and split (in the proportions THETA and (1 − THETA), respectively) into the stock demand for real money by currency and the stock demand for real bonds by currency. In equilibrium these stock demands for real money and real bonds are equal to the respective stock supplies of real money and real bonds by currency, which depend on the stock supply of nominal money by currency and the annual nominal dividend stream from perpetual bonds by currency, the price level by currency, and the nominal long-term interest rate by currency. Since, by definition, the sum of the stock supplies of real money and real bonds by currency is the stock supply of real FA's by currency, it also follows that the stock supply of real FA's by currency equals the stock demand for real FA's by currency (and, therefore, also by country) in equilibrium.

Country A's stock demand for real FA's = QA * (100 + RST).
Country B's stock demand for real FA's = QB * (100 + RST).
Country C's stock demand for real FA's = QC * (100 + RST).

Country A's stock demand for real FA's in Currency A
        = .8 * Country A's stock demand for real FA's.
Country B's stock demand for real FA's in Currency A
        = .4 * Country B's stock demand for real FA's.
Country C's stock demand for real FA's in Currency A
        = .1 * Country C's stock demand for real FA's.

Country A's stock demand for real FA's in Currency B
        = .1 * Country A's stock demand for real FA's.
Country B's stock demand for real FA's in Currency B
        = .4 * Country B's stock demand for real FA's.

Country C's stock demand for real FA's in Currency B
= .1 * Country C's stock demand for real FA's.

Country A's stock demand for real FA's in Currency C
= .1 * Country A's stock demand for real FA's.
Country B's stock demand for real FA's in Currency C
= .2 * Country B's stock demand for real FA's.
Country C's stock demand for real FA's in Currency C
= .8 * Country C's stock demand for real FA's.

Global stock demand for real FA's in Currency A
= Country A's stock demand for real FA's in Currency A
+ Country B's stock demand for real FA's in Currency A
+ Country C's stock demand for real FA's in Currency A.
Global stock demand for real FA's in Currency B
= Country A's stock demand for real FA's in Currency B
+ Country B's stock demand for real FA's in Currency B
+ Country C's stock demand for real FA's in Currency B.
Global stock demand for real FA's in Currency C
= Country A's stock demand for real FA's in Currency C
+ Country B's stock demand for real FA's in Currency C
+ Country C's stock demand for real FA's in Currency C.

Global stock demand for real money in Currency A
= THETA * Global stock demand for real FA's in Currency A.
Global stock demand for real money in Currency B
= THETA * Global stock demand for real FA's in Currency B.
Global stock demand for real money in Currency C
= THETA * Global stock demand for real FA's in Currency C.

Real (global) stock supply of money in Currency A = MSA/PA.
Real (global) stock supply of money in Currency B = MSB/PB.
Real (global) stock supply of money in Currency C = MSC/PC.

Real global stock supply of money in Currency A
= Real global stock demand for money in Currency A.
Real global stock supply of money in Currency B
= Real global stock demand for money in Currency B.
Real global stock supply of money in Currency C
= Real global stock demand for money in Currency C.

Global stock demand for real bonds in Currency A
= (1 − THETA) * Global stock demand for real FA's
in Currency A.
Global stock demand for real bonds in Currency B
= (1 − THETA) * Global stock demand for real FA's
in Currency B.
Global stock demand for real bonds in Currency C
= (1 − THETA) * Global stock demand for real FA's
in Currency C.

Real (global) stock supply of bonds in Currency A
= ((100 * DSA)/(ILTA * PA)).
Real (global) stock supply of bonds in Currency B
= ((100 * DSB)/(ILTB * PB)).
Real (global) stock supply of bonds in Currency C
= ((100 * DSC)/(ILTC * PC)).

Real global stock supply of perpetual bonds in Currency A
= Real global stock demand for perpetual bonds
in Currency A.
Real global stock supply of perpetual bonds in Currency B
= Real global stock demand for perpetual bonds
in Currency B.
Real global stock supply of perpetual bonds in Currency C
= Real global stock demand for perpetual bonds
in Currency C.

Global stock supply of real FA's in Currency A
= MSA/PA + ((100 * DSA)/(ILTA * PA)).
Global stock supply of real FA's in Currency B
= MSB/PB + ((100 * DSB)/(ILTB * PB)).
Global stock supply of real FA's in Currency C
= MSC/PC + ((100 * DSC)/(ILTC * PC)).

Global real stock demand for FA's in Currency A
= Global real stock supply of FA's in Currency A.
Global real stock demand for FA's in Currency B
= Global real stock supply of FA's in Currency B.
Global real stock demand for FA's in Currency C
= Global real stock supply of FA's in Currency C.

Real stock demand by Country A for FA's in Currency A
= (10/7) * Global real stock demand for FA's in Currency A.
Real stock demand by Country B for FA's in Currency A
= (− 1/3) * Global real stock demand for FA's in Currency A.
Real stock demand by Country C for FA's in Currency A
= (− 2/21) * Global real stock demand for FA's in Currency A.

Real stock demand by Country A for FA's in Currency B
= (− 10/7) * Global real stock demand for FA's in Currency B.
Real stock demand by Country B for FA's in Currency B
= 3 * Global real stock demand for FA's in Currency B.
Real stock demand by Country C for FA's in Currency B
= (− 4/7) * Global real stock demand for FA's in Currency B.

Real stock demand by Country A for FA's in Currency C
= 0.0 * Global real stock demand for FA's in Currency C.
Real stock demand by Country B for FA's in Currency C
= (− 1/3) * Global real stock demand for FA's in Currency C.
Real stock demand by Country C for FA's in Currency C
= (4/3) * Global real stock demand for FA's in Currency C.

Global stock demand for real FA's by Country A
= Country A's stock demand for real FA's in Currency A
+ Country A's stock demand for real FA's in Currency B
+ Country A's stock demand for real FA's in Currency C.
Global stock demand for real FA's by Country B
= Country B's stock demand for real FA's in Currency A
+ Country B's stock demand for real FA's in Currency B
+ Country B's stock demand for real FA's in Currency C.
Global stock demand for real FA's by Country C
= Country C's stock demand for real FA's in Currency A
+ Country C's stock demand for real FA's in Currency B
+ Country C's stock demand for real FA's in Currency C.

Real investment by Country A = 35 − .4 * RLTA.
Real investment by Country B = 35 − .4 * RLTB.
Real investment by Country C = 35 − .4 * RLTC.

Real saving by Country A = − 5 + .1 * QA.
Real saving by Country B = − 5 + .1 * QB.
Real saving by Country C = − 5 + .1 * QC.

Real saving by Country A + Real saving by Country B + Real saving by Country C = Real investment by Country A + Real investment by Country B + Real investment by Country C.

Real saving in Currency A by Country A
= .8 * Real saving by Country A.
Real saving in Currency A by Country B
= .4 * Real saving by Country B.
Real saving in Currency A by Country C
= .1 * Real saving by Country C.

Real saving in Currency B by Country A
= .1 * Real saving by Country A.
Real saving in Currency B by Country B
= .4 * Real saving by Country B.
Real saving in Currency B by Country C
= .1 * Real saving by Country C.

Real saving in Currency C by Country A
= .1 * Real saving by Country A.
Real saving in Currency C by Country B
= .2 * Real saving by Country B.
Real saving in Currency C by Country C
= .8 * Real saving by Country C.

Real saving in Currency A
= Real saving in Currency A by Country A
+ Real saving in Currency A by Country B
+ Real saving in Currency A by Country C.
Real saving in Currency B
= Real saving in Currency B by Country A
+ Real saving in Currency B by Country B
+ Real saving in Currency B by Country C.
Real saving in Currency C
= Real saving in Currency C by Country A
+ Real saving in Currency C by Country B
+ Real saving in Currency C by Country C.

Nominal saving in Currency A = Real saving in Currency A
* Average price level in Currency A during period.

Nominal saving in Currency B = Real saving in Currency B
  * Average price level in Currency B during period.
Nominal saving in Currency C = Real saving in Currency C
  * Average price level in Currency C during period.

Nominal saving in Currency A
  = Nominal value of net newly acquired money in Currency A
  + Nominal value of net newly acquired bonds in Currency A.
Nominal saving in Currency B
  = Nominal value of net newly acquired money in Currency B
  + Nominal value of net newly acquired bonds in Currency B.
Nominal saving in Currency C
  = Nominal value of net newly acquired money in Currency C
  + Nominal value of net newly acquired bonds in Currency C.

Change during the period in the annual nominal dividend stream from perpetual bonds in Currency A = (Nominal long-term interest rate in Currency A, average over period)/100 * Net new issue during the period of perpetual bonds in Currency A (measured in terms of nominal principal value).

Change during the period in the annual nominal dividend stream from perpetual bonds in Currency B = (Nominal long-term interest rate in Currency B, average over period)/100 * Net new issue during the period of perpetual bonds in Currency B (measured in terms of nominal principal value).

Change during the period in the annual nominal dividend stream from perpetual bonds in Currency C = (Nominal long-term interest rate in Currency C, average over period)/100 * Net new issue during the period of perpetual bonds in Currency C (measured in terms of nominal principal value).

Actual inflation rate in Currency A
              = Expected inflation rate in Currency A.
Actual inflation rate in Currency B
              = Expected inflation rate in Currency B.
Actual inflation rate in Currency C
              = Expected inflation rate in Currency C.

Actual rate of exchange rate change between Currencies A and B = Expected rate of exchange rate change between Currencies A and B.

Actual rate of exchange rate change between currencies A and C = Expected rate of exchange rate change between Currencies A and C.

Global stock supply of nominal money in Currency A (end of period) = Global stock supply of nominal money in Currency A (start of period) + Change during the period in the global stock supply of nominal money in Currency A.

Global stock supply of nominal money in Currency B (end of period) = Global stock supply of nominal money in Currency B (start of period) + Change during the period in the global stock supply of nominal money in Currency B.

Global stock supply of nominal money in Currency C (end of period) = Global stock supply of nominal money in Currency C (start of period) + Change during the period in the global stock supply of nominal money in Currency C.

In the next three formulas the term due to the financing of the government budget deficit would not apply to the present version of the 3C model, which has no fiscal policy:

Net new issue during the period of nominal money in Currency A = Net new issue due to private capital formation + Net new issue due to financing of government budget deficits + Net new issue due to central bank money-bond operations + Net new issue due to central bank foreign exchange operations.

Net new issue during the period of nominal money in Currency B = Net new issue due to private capital formation + Net new issue due to financing of government budget deficits + Net new issue due to central bank money-bond operations + Net new issue due to central bank foreign exchange operations.

Net new issue during the period of nominal money in Currency C = Net new issue due to private capital formation + Net new issue due to financing of government budget deficits + Net new issue due to central bank money-bond operations + Net new issue due to central bank foreign exchange operations.

Annual nominal dividend stream from global stock supply of perpetual bonds in Currency A (end of period) = Annual nominal dividend stream from global stock supply of perpetual bonds in Currency A (start of period) + Change during the period in the annual nominal dividend stream from global stock supply of perpetual bonds in Currency A.

Annual nominal dividend stream from global stock supply of perpetual bonds in Currency B (end of period) = Annual nominal dividend stream from global stock supply of perpetual bonds in Currency B (start of period) + Change during the period in the annual nominal dividend stream from global stock supply of perpetual bonds in Currency B.

Annual nominal dividend stream from global stock supply of perpetual bonds in Currency C (end of period) = Annual nominal dividend stream from global stock supply of perpetual bonds in Currency C (start of period) + Change during the period in the annual nominal dividend stream from global stock supply of perpetual bonds in Currency C.

In the next three formulas the term due to the financing of the government budget deficit would not apply to the present version of the 3C model, which has no fiscal policy:

Net new issue during the period of perpetual bonds in Currency A (measured in terms of nominal principal value) = Net new issue due to private capital formation + Net new issue due to financing of government budget deficits + Net new issue due to central bank money-bond operations.

Net new issue during the period of perpetual bonds in Currency B (measured in terms of nominal principal value) = Net new issue due to private capital formation + Net new issue due to financing of government budget deficits + Net new issue due to central bank money-bond operations.

Net new issue during the period of perpetual bonds in Currency C (measured in terms of nominal principal value) = Net new issue due to private capital formation + Net new issue due to financing of government budget deficits + Net new issue due to central bank money-bond operations.

In the 3C model with floating exchange rates the linking equations (one for each currency) are:

$$\text{MSDELA} + \text{BDELA} = \text{SURA} * \text{PAVGA},$$
$$\text{MSDELB} + \text{BDELB} = \text{SURB} * \text{PAVGB},$$
$$\text{MSDELC} + \text{BDELC} = \text{SURC} * \text{PAVGC}.$$

In the 3C model with fixed exchange rates the linking equations (one for each currency) are:

$$\text{MLNFXA} + \text{BDELA} = \text{SURA} * \text{PAVGA},$$
$$\text{MLNFXB} + \text{BDELB} = \text{SURB} * \text{PAVGB},$$
$$\text{MLNFXC} + \text{BDELC} = \text{SURC} * \text{PAVGC}.$$

5. International Accounts and Exchange Rates

Under flexible exchange rates the central bank neither buys nor sells foreign exchange and, therefore, the balance of payments is zero. Because the government will not intervene, all adjustments in the real supply of money must occur through price changes or the trading of nominal money between private holders. (If the 3C model also had government debt, then the debt service payments might affect the money supply. See the note at the end of Section 3 in Chapter 2.)

Under fixed exchange rates, the central bank undertakes to buy and sell foreign money in whatever amounts are necessary to maintain the fixed exchange rates. These rates may, if the authorities desire, vary from period to period.

Under fixed exchange rates a country has a balance of payments surplus if its foreign exchange reserves have increased. The counterpart of official purchases of foreign exchange is, of course, official sales of domestic currency. The domestic currency may be sold to foreigners who wish to hold it or buy domestic perpetual bonds or goods with it or to domestic residents who do not wish to hold foreign currency but who may have obtained it by having sold foreign bonds and goods.

Viewed in any single currency, the total inventories of the

central bank never change, because decreases in one money are made up by exactly offsetting increases in another. In the international model with fixed exchange rates, the net sales of money in the various currencies by the foreign exchange authorities during the period are described by the foreign exchange equation, which is expressed (arbitrarily) in Currency A:

MLFXA + (KAVG * MLFXB) + (HAVG * MLFXC) = 0,

or, in words,

(Net sales of Currency A by the foreign exchange authorities during the period) + ((Average exchange rate of Currency B, expressed in terms of Currency A, during the period) * (Net sales of Currency B by the foreign exchange authorities during the period)) + ((Average exchange rate of Currency C, expressed in terms of Currency A, during the period) * (Net sales of Currency C by the foreign exchange authorities during the period)) = 0.

In equilibrium the stock demand for real FA's equals the stock supply of real FA's in each currency. For each currency, adjustment to (potential or incipient) disequilibrium proceeds by swapping of money and bonds, or money and foreign money, or money and goods among different holders; then, when such exchanges have ceased, adjustment proceeds by changes in the real stocks of money and perpetual bonds by means of changes in the price level and the nominal long-term interest rate. The price level and the nominal long-term interest rate in each currency equate the stock demand for and the stock supply of real money and real perpetual bonds, respectively, in each currency, and by implication the stock demand for and the stock supply of real goods in each currency, which goods remain present but backstage in the scenes of the model.

In order to equate supply and demand for money and bonds in each currency, individuals may swap money and bonds, money and goods, or money in different currencies. If this swapping crosses national borders, then international accounts register the transactions as follows.

If there is no government sector,

$$BTARL = SUNA - INVRLA,$$
$$BTBRL = SUNB - INVRLB,$$
$$BTCRL = SUNC = INVRLC,$$

$$BPANLA = MLFXA,$$
$$BPBNLB = MLFXB,$$
$$BPCNLC = MLFXC,$$

$$BPARL = BPANLA/PAVGA,$$
$$BPBRL = BPBNLB/PAVGB,$$
$$BPCRL = BPCNLC/PAVGC,$$

$$BCARL = BPARL - BTARL,$$
$$BCBRL = BPBRL - BRBRL,$$
$$BCCRL = BPCRL - BTCRL.$$

(Note: For floating rates $MLFXA = 0.0, MLFXB = 0.0, MLFXC = 0.0$.)

The balance of trade (BT), balance of payments (BP), and balance on capital account (BC) for countries A, B, and C are each measured in real terms in the formulas above. To express any such real measure in nominal terms in currencies A, B, or C, multiply by PAVGA, PAVGB, or PAVGC, respectively.

Notice that:

1. the sum of the balances of trade over all countries is zero, in real terms and in each currency;
2. the sum of the balances of payments over all countries is zero, in real terms and in each currency;
3. the sum of the balances on capital account over all countries is zero, in real terms and in each currency.

Note: Because all international payments flows take place, in this model, in equilibrium, deficits in the balance of trade and/ or the balance of payments do not represent a disequilibrium situation.

Note: The international payments accounts may be measured in terms of various currencies, but this does not mean that the actual transactions took place in these currencies. Thus, the same transactions, regardless of the original currencies in which they were transacted, may be aggregated and expressed in real terms or in any of the three currencies.

6

The 3C International Model: Simulation Results

1. 3C Simulation Notes

The solution process for the international model makes use of two facts: (a) in equilibrium real short-term interest rates are the same for all three currencies; (b) world exports and world imports are equal. Arbitrary values of RST are chosen and the model is solved for each. Each solution contains values for real investment and real saving by country. The equilibrium value of RST is that which equalizes total real investment for the world and total real saving for the world. Or, more accurately, equalizes total world imports and total world imports.

At the end of each period the stock supply of real money and real perpetual bonds can be calculated for each currency. From the real financial asset demands in each currency (equal in equilibrium to these supplies) the common value of RST and the three real outputs for each country are simultaneously determined. The values of RST and real output determine whether for each country the solution in that period is a RHS solution or a LHS solution. In Simulations 6–9, Countries A and C have LHS solutions for each period but Country B has RHS solutions in some periods and LHS solutions in others. The existence of RHS solutions in some periods does not seem to cause any instabilities in these simulation examples as it appears to in the 1C model.

In the 3C simulations of a devaluation, K and H are

maintained at constant values at the starts of Periods 1–3, then changed to different constant values for the starts of Periods 4–6. (The values of K and H at the start of Period 1 are not controllable in Period 1, but the values at the starts of Periods 2 and 3, which are controllable by actions in Periods 1 and 2, respectively, are set equal to the values at the start of Period 1.)

Devaluations are gradual in the 3C model. The exchange rates change smoothly during Period 3 from the old official value at the start of Period 3 to the new official value at the start of Period 4 (the end of Period 3). This gradualism is a necessary consequence of having an equilibrium model. If the change were sudden, say, in that imaginary picosecond between the end of Period 3 and the start of Period 4, the prices and exchange rates would either have to readjust instantly or violate the purchasing power parity equations. Neither possibility is consistent with equilibrium. Therefore, the change in exchange rates must be made smoothly over the course of the period.

In the 3C simulations (Simulations 6–9), although real investment is roughly equal for the three countries, real saving is much higher in Country B than in Countries A and C. This asymmetry in the solutions probably results from the choice of parameters in the currency preference matrix (and its inverse). Aside from these parameters, both the 3C floating and fixed exchange rate models are symmetrical in their economic equations. (The values of the exogenous variables also could cause this asymmetry, but it is unlikely since they are not very different from currency to currency.) Another source of asymmetry could be the solution routines. The 3C floating exchange rate program is symmetrical. Although the 3C fixed exchange rate program is asymmetrical, it cannot be the source of the asymmetry in the solution because the asymmetry is different. In the 3C fixed exchange rate program, it is Currency A that is treated differently from Currencies B and C.

As the 3C fixed exchange rate simulations (Simulations 7–9) show, a balance of payments deficit can be a feature of a continuing adjustment in a dynamic equilibrium rather than an inevitable symptom of disequilibrium. That is, the equality of the stock demand for real money and the stock supply of real money is no barrier to having a balance of payments deficit.

Since a balance of payments deficit does not necessarily signify disequilibrium, one might wonder whether a devaluation—often said to represent an attempt to restore equilibrium—would help to rectify a deficit. From the simulation results it appears that the devaluations have little such effect once the exchange rate stabilizes (i.e., after Period 3).

In the 3C model consistency between the 3C floating rate program and the 3C fixed rate program implies that when the fixed rate program is run with the exchange rates pegged to the rates shown under the floating exchange rate regime in Simulation 6, that the amount of official intervention required (and the balance of payments for each country) should be exactly zero. Given the imprecise tolerances involved, the amount of intervention required is, in fact, gratifyingly small.

From period to period the 1C model with control variable MSDEL has the potential for attaining either a LHS solution or a RHS solution. With control variable Q the 1C model has no such freedom. It appears that the 3C model may sometimes have no such freedom, as in Simulations 6–9. Whether this is generally true is open to question.

Real exports for the world equals real imports for the world, where real exports for the world equals the sum of exports from the three countries, and real imports for the world equals the sum of imports into the three countries.

Real saving for the world equals real investment for the world, where real saving for the world equals the total of real saving in the three countries, and real investment for the world equals the total of real investment in the three countries. The foregoing relationship is true if the fiscal policy variables (net) tax revenues, government purchases, and government debt service are all equal to zero for each country. However, if, for one (or more) countries, one (or more) of these fiscal policy variables is (are) not zero, the relationship above must be modified to be that the sum of real saving (both from production and from debt service payments on government debt held by the public) for the world plus the sum of real (net) tax revenues for the world equals the sum of real investment for the world plus the sum of real government purchases for the world plus the sum of government debt service payments to the public for the world. Or, combining a few terms: the sum of real saving (both from production and from debt service payments on government debt held by the public) for the world equals the sum of real investment for the world plus the sum of real government budget deficits for the world. The subject of how fiscal policy variables might fit into an international model is discussed in Appendix 5. The inclusion of fiscal policy into the closed-country model will be discussed in Chapter 7, where the 1C(F) model is introduced.

In the 3C model it might be possible to pursue any combination of the 1C targets. Thus, one currency might target ILTNXT, a second PDOTE, and a third MSNXT. It is not obvious to me how to determine whether a given set of targets is consistent, other than by examining each case. (I feel there should be an easier way based on degrees of freedom or some such idea.)

2. 3C Variables

List of Variable Names for 3C Model (Floating Exchange Rates) Shown in Simulation 6, Tables 1–3

(Note: These names lack the final A, B, or C.)

MS = (global) nominal money supply by currency, start of period.

MSDEL = change in (global) nominal money supply by currency during period.

DS = annual (global) nominal dividend stream from perpetual bonds by currency, start of period.

SUN = real saving by country during period.

INVRL = real investment by country during period.

Q = real output by country during period.

FUN = real FA stock demand by country, start of period.

P = price level in each currency, start of period.

ILT = nominal long-term interest rate in each currency, start of period.

PDOTE = expected rate of price change in each currency during period.

PAVG = price level in each currency, average over period.

SAVNL = nominal saving in each currency during period.

BDEL = nominal principal value of perpetual bonds (net) newly issued in each currency during period.

ILTAV = nominal long-term interest rate in each currency, average over period.

DSDEL = change in annual nominal dividend stream from perpetual bonds by currency during period.

IST = nominal short-term interest rate in each currency, start of period.

RLT = real long-term interest rate in each currency, start of period.

SUR = real saving by currency during period.

FUR = real FA stock demand by currency, start of period.

List of Variable Names for 3C Model (Fixed Exchange Rates) Shown in Simulations 7–9, Tables 1–3

(Note: These names lack the final A, B, or C.)

MS = (global) nominal money supply by currency, start of period.

MLTOT = change in (global) nominal money supply by currency during period.

DS = annual (global) nominal dividend stream from perpetual bonds by currency, start of period.

SUN = real saving by country during period.

INVRL = real investment by country during period.

Q = real output by country during period.

FUN = real FA stock demand by country, start of period.

P = price level in each currency, start of period.

ILT = nominal long-term interest rate in each currency, start of period.

PDOTE = expected rate of price change in each currency during period.

PAVG = price level in each currency, average over period.

SAVNL = nominal saving in each currency during period.

BDEL = nominal principal value of perpetual bonds (net) newly issued in each currency during period.

ILTAV = nominal long-term interest rate in each currency, average over period.

DSDEL = change in annual nominal dividend stream from perpetual bonds by currency during period.

IST = nominal short-term interest rate in each currency, start of period.

RLT = real long-term interest rate in each currency, start of period.

SUR = real saving by currency during period.

FUR = real FA stock demand by currency, start of period.

MLNFX = portion of change in (global) nominal money supply by currency not due to foreign exchange operations, start of period.

MLFX = portion of change in (global) nominal money supply by currency due to foreign exchange operations, start of period.

Note: The variable MLTOT in the 3C fixed exchange rate model is similar to MSDEL in the 3C floating exchange rate model, the difference being that MLTOT is the sum of two components, MLNFX and MLFX.

List of Variable Names for 3C Models (Floating and Fixed Exchange Rates) Not Shown in Simulations 6–9, Tables 1–3

(Note: These names lack the final A, B, or C.)

MSNXT = (global) nominal money supply by currency, end of period.

PNXT = price level in each currency, end of period.

ILTNX = nominal long-term interest rate in each currency, end of period.

DSNXT = annual (global) nominal dividend stream from perpetual bonds by currency, end of period.

PDOT = actual rate of price change in each currency realized during period.

List of Variable Names for 3C Model (Floating or Fixed) Shown in Simulations 6–9, Table 4

RST = real short-term interest rate in each currency, start of period.

K = exchange rate between Currency A and Currency B, start of period.

H = exchange rate between Currency A and Currency C, start of period.

KDOTE = expected rate of change during period of exchange rate between Currencies A and B.

HDOTE = expected rate of change during period of exchange rate between Currencies A and C.

KAVG = average exchange rate during period between Currencies A and B.

HAVG = average exchange rate during period between Currencies A and C.

List of Variable Names for 3C Model (Floating or Fixed) Not Shown in Simulations 6–9, Table 4

KNXT = exchange rate between Currency A and Currency B, end of period.

HNXT = exchange rate between Currency A and Currency C, end of period.

KDOT = actual rate of change during period of exchange rate between Currencies A and B.

HDOT = actual rate of change during period of exchange rate between Currencies A and C.

List of Variable Names for 3C Model (Floating or Fixed) Shown in Simulations 6–9, Table 5

BTARL = balance of trade of Country A measured in real terms.

BTBRL = balance of trade of Country B measured in real terms.

BTCRL = balance of trade of Country C measured in real terms.

BPARL = balance of payments of Country A measured in real terms.

BPBRL = balance of payments of Country B measured in real terms.

BPCRL = balance of payments of Country C measured in real terms.

BCARL = balance on capital account of Country A measured in real terms.

BCBRL = balance on capital account of Country B measured in real terms.

BCCRL = balance on capital account of Country C measured in real terms.

List of Variable Names for 3C Model (Floating or Fixed) Shown in Simulations 6–9, Table 6

BTANLA = balance of trade of Country A measured in Currency A.

BTBNLA = balance of trade of Country B measured in Currency A.

BTCNLA = balance of trade of Country C measured in Currency A.

BPANLA = balance of payments of Country A measured in Currency A.

BPBNLA = balance of payments of Country B measured in Currency A.

BPCNLA = balance of payments of Country C measured in Currency A.

BCANLA = balance on capital account of Country A measured in Currency A.

BCBNLA = balance on capital account of Country B measured in Currency A.

BCCNLA = balance on capital account of Country C measured in Currency A.

List of Variable Names for 3C Model (Floating or Fixed) Shown in Simulations 6–9, Table 7

BTANLB = balance of trade of Country A measured in Currency B.

BTBNLB = balance of trade of Country B measured in Currency B.

BTCNLB = balance of trade of Country C measured in Currency B.

BPANLB = balance of payments of Country A measured in Currency B.

BPBNLB = balance of payments of Country B measured in Currency B.

BPCNLB = balance of payments of Country C measured in Currency B.

BCANLB = balance on capital account of Country A measured in Currency B.

BCBNLB = balance on capital account of Country B measured in Currency B.

BCCNLB = balance on capital account of Country C measured in Currency B.

List of Variable Names for 3C Model (Floating or Fixed) Shown in Simulations 6–9, Table 8

BTANLC = balance of trade of Country A measured in Currency C.

BTBNLC = balance of trade of Country B measured in Currency C.

BTCNLC = balance of trade of Country C measured in Currency C.

BPANLC = balance of payments of Country A measured in Currency C.

BPBNLC = balance of payments of Country B measured in Currency C.

BPCNLC = balance of payments of Country C measured in Currency C.

BCANLC = balance on capital account of Country A measured in Currency C.

BCBNLC = balance on capital account of Country B measured in Currency C.

BCCNLC = balance on capital account of Country C measured in Currency C.

3. Tables for 3C Simulations 6–9

This section contains tables for Simulations 6–9, numerical examples of the 3C model. In the simulation tables (Tables 1–3 of Simulation 6 and Tables 1–4 of Simulations 7–9) the values in italics are exogenous. In Table 5 of Simulation 6 the values in italics are constrained, by the model's structure, to be zero.

Simulation 6, 3C Floating (LHS), Table 1 of 8.

Scenario: No official intervention in the foreign exchange market.

Variable	Period 1	Period 2	Period 3	Period 4	Period 5	Period 6
MSA	*2010.00000*	2040.00000	2075.00000	2115.00000	2160.00000	2210.00000
MSDELA	*30.00000*	35.00000	40.00000	45.00000	50.00000	0.00000
DSA	*800.00000*	789.04170	776.57413	762.74040	747.70280	731.63420
SUNA	1.29602	1.69175	1.62712	1.29144	0.83864	0.00000
INVRLA	17.65157	19.41787	20.54040	21.35957	22.09106	0.00000
QA	62.96019	66.91754	66.27126	62.91439	58.38642	0.00000
FUNA	9214.27983	9523.09991	9270.62199	8696.05658	7984.49120	0.00000
PA	*0.10000*	0.09752	0.09732	0.09823	0.09967	0.10143
ILTA	39.80100	38.67851	37.42526	36.06338	34.61587	33.10562
PDOTEA	−2.49010	−0.19921	0.93740	1.46329	1.77173	0.00000
PAVGA	0.09875	0.09742	0.09778	0.09895	0.10054	0.00000
SAVNLA	2.07063	2.23088	2.34492	2.43942	2.53324	0.00000
BDELA	−27.92937	−32.76912	−37.65508	−42.56058	−47.46676	0.00000
ILTAVA	39.23574	38.04673	36.73801	35.33221	33.85232	0.00000
DSDELA	−10.95830	−12.46758	−13.83373	−15.03760	−16.06860	0.00000
ISTA	42.70307	42.02720	41.20162	40.24500	39.17779	0.00000
RLTA	43.37107	38.95533	36.14900	34.10109	32.27236	0.00000
SURA	20.96823	22.89954	23.98223	24.65373	25.19565	0.00000
FURA	40200.01438	41838.79804	42641.31786	43060.84545	43344.62686	43578.14126

Simulation 6, 3C Floating (LHS), Table 2 of 8.

Scenario: No official intervention in the foreign exchange market.

Variable	Period 1	Period 2	Period 3	Period 4	Period 5	Period 6
MSB	2025.00000	2075.00000	2120.00000	2160.00000	2195.00000	2225.00000
MSDELB	50.00000	45.00000	40.00000	35.00000	30.00000	0.00000
DSB	790.00000	771.86211	756.39889	743.31975	732.39776	723.45619
SUNB	48.83182	52.79159	55.62531	58.00906	60.31559	0.00000
INVRLB	18.44477	19.78917	20.52201	20.97252	21.35302	0.00000
QB	538.31836	577.91611	606.25335	630.09084	653.15608	0.00000
FUNB	78783.37471	82243.80615	84808.18977	87091.44761	89320.75618	0.00000
PB	0.12000	0.11799	0.11728	0.11684	0.11627	0.11563
ILTB	39.01235	37.19817	35.67919	34.41295	33.36664	32.51489
PDOTEB	-1.68029	-0.60054	-0.37871	-0.48550	-0.55982	0.00000
PAVGB	0.11899	0.11764	0.11706	0.11656	0.11595	0.00000
SAVNLB	2.38707	2.55450	2.67406	2.76820	2.85336	0.00000
BDELB	-47.61293	-42.44550	-37.32594	-32.23180	-27.14664	0.00000
ILTAVB	38.09446	36.43077	35.04035	33.88576	32.93801	0.00000
DSDELB	-18.13789	-15.46322	-13.07914	-10.92199	-8.94156	0.00000
ISTB	43.88939	41.45550	39.35874	37.54875	35.98623	0.00000
RLTB	41.38807	38.02709	36.19497	35.06871	34.11746	0.00000
SURB	20.06101	21.71532	22.84325	23.74972	24.60860	0.00000
FURB	33750.01542	35172.62493	36151.87937	36973.60294	37755.48035	38486.32783

Simulation 6, 3C Floating (LHS), Table 3 of 8.

Scenario: No official intervention in the foreign exchange market.

Variable	Period 1	Period 2	Period 3	Period 4	Period 5	Period 6
MSC	2040.00000	2080.00000	2120.00000	2160.00000	2200.00000	2240.00000
MSDELC	40.00000	40.00000	40.00000	40.00000	40.00000	0.00000
DSC	840.00000	824.62799	809.88375	795.71195	782.07204	768.93328
SUNC	3.98687	4.29508	4.30409	4.16953	3.98504	0.00000
INVRLC	18.01871	19.57491	20.50319	21.13906	21.69720	0.00000
QC	89.86873	92.95079	93.04094	91.69537	89.85048	0.00000
FUNC	13152.36927	13227.91832	13015.40640	12674.17631	12287.28200	0.00000
PC	0.15000	0.14866	0.14982	0.15197	0.15443	0.15708
ILTC	41.17647	39.64558	38.20206	36.83852	35.54873	34.32738
PDOTEC	−0.89627	0.78149	1.43864	1.62356	1.71978	0.00000
PAVGC	0.14933	0.14924	0.15089	0.15319	0.15575	0.00000
SAVNLC	1.95403	2.11373	2.22275	2.30808	2.38836	0.00000
BDELC	−38.04597	−37.88627	−37.77725	−37.69192	−37.61164	0.00000
ILTAVC	40.40377	38.91713	37.51410	36.18788	34.93272	0.00000
DSDELC	−15.37201	−14.74425	−14.17179	−13.63991	−13.13877	0.00000
ISTC	45.03792	43.42420	41.90348	40.46674	39.10668	0.00000
RLTC	42.45324	38.56273	36.24203	34.65236	33.25700	0.00000
SURC	13.08546	14.16355	14.73105	15.06658	15.33502	0.00000
	27200.00432	27983.41202	28301.03145	28427.24239	28492.43207	28521.40233

Simulation 6, 3C Floating (LHS), Table 4 of 8.

Scenario: No official intervention in the foreign exchange market.

Variable	Period 1	Period 2	Period 3	Period 4	Period 5	Period 6
RST	46.35090	42.31098	39.88903	38.22046	36.75254	0.00000
K	0.83333	0.82649	0.82982	0.84075	0.85716	0.87720
H	0.66667	0.65598	0.64961	0.64641	0.64539	0.64572
KDOTE	−0.82447	0.40416	1.32240	1.96021	2.34697	0.00000
HDOTE	−1.60982	−0.97403	−0.49460	−0.15786	0.05112	0.00000
KAVG	0.82990	0.82815	0.83526	0.84892	0.86713	0.00000
HAVG	0.66130	0.65279	0.64801	0.64590	0.64556	0.00000

Simulation 6, 3C Floating (LHS), Table 5 of 8.

Scenario: No official intervention in the foreign exchange market.

Variable	Period 1	Period 2	Period 3	Period 4	Period 5
BTARL	−16.35556	−17.72612	−18.91328	−20.06813	−21.25242
BTBRL	30.38704	33.00242	35.10330	37.03654	38.96257
BTCRL	−14.03184	−15.27983	−16.19910	−16.96952	−17.71216
BPARL	0.00000	0.00000	0.00000	0.00000	0.00000
BPBRL	0.00000	0.00000	0.00000	0.00000	0.00000
BPCRL	0.00000	0.00000	0.00000	0.00000	0.00000
BCARL	16.35556	17.72612	18.91328	20.06813	21.25242
BCBRL	−30.38704	−33.00242	−35.10330	−37.03654	−38.96257
BCCRL	14.03184	15.27983	16.19910	16.96952	17.71216

Simulation 6, 3C Floating (LHS), Table 6 of 8.

Scenario: No official intervention in the foreign exchange market.

Variable	Period 1	Period 2	Period 3	Period 4	Period 5
BTANLA	−1.61512	−1.72688	−1.84929	−1.98568	−2.13678
BTBNLA	3.00074	3.21510	3.43230	3.66466	3.91741
BTCNLA	−1.38565	−1.48857	−1.58390	−1.67909	−1.78083
BPANLA	0.00000	0.00000	0.00000	0.00000	0.00000
BPBNLA	0.00000	0.00000	0.00000	0.00000	0.00000
BPCNLA	0.00000	0.00000	0.00000	0.00000	0.00000
BCANLA	1.61512	1.72688	1.84929	1.98568	2.13678
BCBNLA	−3.00074	−3.21510	−3.43230	−3.66466	−3.91741
BCCNLA	1.38565	1.48857	1.58390	1.67909	1.78083

Simulation 6, 3C Floating (LHS), Table 7 of 8.

Scenario: No official intervention in the foreign exchange market.

Variable	Period 1	Period 2	Period 3	Period 4	Period 5
BTANLB	−1.94616	−2.08522	−2.21401	−2.33908	−2.46421
BTBNLB	3.61577	3.88226	4.10924	4.31687	4.51769
BTCNLB	−1.66965	−1.79745	−1.89629	−1.97792	−2.05372
BPANLB	0.00000	0.00000	0.00000	0.00000	0.00000
BPBNLB	0.00000	0.00000	0.00000	0.00000	0.00000
BPCNLB	0.00000	0.00000	0.00000	0.00000	0.00000
BCANLB	1.94616	2.08522	2.21401	2.33908	2.46421
BCBNLB	−3.61577	−3.88226	−4.10924	−4.31687	−4.51769

Simulation 6, 3C Floating (LHS), Table 8 of 8.

Scenario: No official intervention in the foreign exchange market.

Variable	Period 1	Period 2	Period 3	Period 4	Period 5
BTANLC	-2.44235	-2.64540	-2.85380	-3.07428	-3.30997
BTBNLC	4.53764	4.92520	5.29669	5.67370	6.06824
BTCNLC	-2.09535	-2.28033	-2.44426	-2.59960	-2.75859
BPANLC	0.00000	0.00000	0.00000	0.00000	0.00000
BPBNLC	0.00000	0.00000	0.00000	0.00000	0.00000
BPCNLC	0.00000	0.00000	0.00000	0.00000	0.00000
BCANLC	2.44235	2.64540	2.85380	3.07428	3.30997
BCBNLC	-4.53764	-4.92520	-5.29669	-5.67370	-6.06824
BCCNLC	2.09535	2.28033	2.44426	2.59960	2.75859

Simulation 7, 3C Fixed (LHS), Table 1 of 8.

Scenario: Official intervention to maintain exchange rates.

Variable	Period 1	Period 2	Period 3	Period 4	Period 5	Period 6
MSA	2010.00000	2040.00000	2075.00000	2115.00000	2160.00000	2210.00000
MLTOTA	30.00000	35.00000	40.00000	45.00000	50.00000	0.00000
DSA	800.00000	781.26995	764.67786	749.81481	736.25349	723.46249
SUNA	1.30697	1.34674	1.40215	1.57635	1.91867	0.00000
INVRLA	18.15796	19.67435	20.61156	21.29388	21.91438	0.00000
QA	63.06968	63.46740	64.02148	65.76351	69.18673	0.00000
FUNA	9214.27983	9027.52298	8955.99503	9090.74657	9464.01743	0.00000
PA	0.10000	0.09838	0.09837	0.09900	0.09988	0.10091
ILTA	39.80100	38.29755	36.85195	35.45224	34.08581	32.73586
PDOTEA	-1.62140	-0.01199	0.64781	0.88403	1.03362	0.00000
PAVGA	0.09919	0.09837	0.09868	0.09944	0.10039	0.00000
SAVNLA	2.08449	2.22882	2.33475	2.42716	2.52185	0.00000
BDELA	-47.97406	-44.16573	-41.12027	-39.01155	-38.29182	0.00000
ILTAVA	39.04203	37.56779	36.14532	34.76231	33.40402	0.00000
DSDELA	-18.73005	-16.59209	-14.86305	-13.56132	-12.79100	0.00000
ISTA	43.72670	42.22027	40.80010	39.46102	38.20958	0.00000
RLTA	42.10509	38.31412	35.97111	34.26530	32.71404	0.00000
SURA	21.01600	22.65692	23.65861	24.40814	25.11955	0.00000
FURA	40200.01438	41472.45045	42189.04432	42725.54554	43252.23899	43800.71328
MLNFXA	50.05855	46.39455	43.45502	41.43871	40.81367	0.00000
MLFXA	-20.05855	-11.39455	-3.45502	3.56129	9.18633	0.00000

Simulation 7, 3C Fixed (LHS), Table 2 of 8.

Scenario: Official intervention to maintain exchange rates.

Variable	Period 1	Period 2	Period 3	Period 4	Period 5	Period 6
MSB	*2025.00000*	2075.00000	2120.00000	2160.00000	2195.00000	2225.00000
MLTOTB	*50.00000*	45.00000	40.00000	35.00000	*30.00000*	0.00000
DSB	*790.00000*	773.04733	752.44291	728.02472	699.58756	666.92282
SUNB	48.92544	52.81724	55.13117	56.59672	57.63287	0.00000
INVRLB	18.47886	20.09130	21.15180	21.98671	22.79090	0.00000
QB	539.25454	578.17260	601.31194	615.96744	626.32887	0.00000
FUNB	78783.37471	82238.54085	84117.80980	85147.58693	85675.20949	0.00000
PB	*0.12000*	0.11805	0.11804	0.11881	0.11986	0.12109
ILTB	39.01235	37.25529	35.49259	33.70485	31.87187	29.97406
PDOTEB	−1.62100	−0.01199	0.64781	0.88403	1.03362	0.00000
PAVGB	0.11902	0.11805	0.11842	0.11933	0.12047	0.00000
SAVNLB	2.39250	2.56331	2.68548	2.78093	2.86443	0.00000
BDELB	−44.46754	−56.66275	−70.59896	−86.76334	−105.68240	0.00000
ILTAVB	38.12370	36.36326	34.58717	32.77555	30.90840	0.00000
DSDELB	−16.95267	−20.60442	−24.41818	−28.43716	−32.66474	0.00000
ISTB	43.72860	42.22169	40.79670	39.45593	38.20338	0.00000
RLTB	41.30286	37.27175	34.62050	32.53322	30.52276	0.00000
SURB	20.10112	21.71420	22.67711	23.30469	23.77648	0.00000
FURB	33750.01542	35153.18135	35919.84481	36362.01990	36627.42363	36748.18792
MLNFXB	46.86004	59.22606	73.28444	89.54427	108.54683	0.00000
MLFXB	3.13996	−14.22606	−33.28444	−54.54427	−78.54683	0.00000

Simulation 7, 3C Fixed (LHS), Table 3 of 8.

Scenario: Official intervention to maintain exchange rates.

Variable	Period 1	Period 2	Period 3	Period 4	Period 5	Period 6
MSC	2040.00000	2080.00000	2120.00000	2160.00000	2200.00000	2240.00000
MLTOTC	40.00000	40.00000	40.00000	40.00000	40.00000	0.00000
DSC	840.00000	835.16721	833.96977	837.49025	847.21090	865.26419
SUNC	4.00250	4.52632	4.84428	5.08370	5.31466	0.00000
INVRLC	17.59841	18.93237	19.62346	19.97734	20.16298	0.00000
QC	90.02502	95.26322	98.44279	100.83704	103.14662	0.00000
FUNC	13152.36927	13550.12082	13771.20756	13939.09830	14109.37434	0.00000
PC	0.15000	0.14757	0.14755	0.14851	0.14982	0.15137
ILTC	41.17647	40.15227	39.33820	38.77270	38.50959	38.62787
PDOTEC	−1.62191	−0.01199	0.64781	0.88403	1.03362	0.00000
PAVGC	0.14878	0.14756	0.14803	0.14916	0.15059	0.00000
SAVNLC	1.95164	2.11291	2.22660	2.31854	2.40495	0.00000
BDELC	−11.88552	−3.01293	9.01428	25.15636	46.80818	0.00000
ILTAVC	40.66115	39.74315	39.05442	38.64092	38.56868	0.00000
DSDELC	−4.83279	−1.19744	3.52047	9.72065	18.05330	0.00000
ISTC	43.72726	42.22169	40.79670	39.45593	38.20338	0.00000
RLTC	43.50398	40.16907	38.44136	37.55666	37.09256	0.00000
SURC	13.11778	14.31918	15.04187	15.54394	15.97017	0.00000
FURC	27200.00432	28190.56330	28736.13379	29089.87704	29368.94955	29597.00848
MLNFXC	13.83717	5.12585	−6.78768	−22.83782	−44.40323	0.00000
MLFXC	26.16283	34.87415	46.78768	62.83782	84.40323	0.00000

Simulation 7, 3C Fixed (LHS), Table 4 of 8.

Scenario: Official intervention to maintain exchange rates.

Variable	Period 1	Period 2	Period 3	Period 4	Period 5	Period 6
RST	46.09682	42.23874	39.89047	38.23391	36.78949	0.00000
K	0.83333	0.83333	0.83333	0.83333	0.83333	0.83333
H	0.66667	0.66667	0.66667	0.66667	0.66667	0.66667
KDOTE	−0.00132	−0.00100	0.00241	0.00365	0.00448	0.00000
HDOTE	−0.00039	−0.00100	0.00241	0.00365	0.00448	0.00000
KAVG	0.83333	0.83333	0.83333	0.83333	0.83333	0.00000
HAVG	0.66667	0.66667	0.66667	0.66667	0.66667	0.00000

Simulation 7, 3C Fixed (LHS), Table 5 of 8.

Scenario: Official intervention to maintain exchange rates.

Variable	Period 1	Period 2	Period 3	Period 4	Period 5
BTARL	−16.85100	−18.32761	−19.20941	−19.71753	−19.99571
BTBRL	30.44658	32.72594	33.97937	34.61001	34.84197
BTCRL	−13.59591	−14.40605	−14.77918	−14.89364	−14.84832
BPARL	−202.23182	−115.83044	−35.01065	35.81318	91.50269
BPBRL	26.38101	−120.51112	−281.06557	−457.09047	−651.98490
BPCRL	175.85081	236.34157	316.07622	421.27729	560.48222
BCARL	−185.38082	−97.50283	−15.80124	55.53072	111.49840
BCBRL	−4.06557	−153.23706	−315.04494	−491.70048	−686.82687
BCCRL	189.44672	250.74762	330.85540	436.17093	575.33053

Simulation 7, 3C Fixed (LHS), Table 6 of 8.

Scenario: Official intervention to maintain exchange rates.

Variable	Period 1	Period 2	Period 3	Period 4	Period 5
BTANLA	−1.67138	−1.80294	−1.89568	−1.96072	−2.00745
BTBNLA	3.01987	3.21934	3.35325	3.44164	3.49793
BTCNLA	−1.34852	−1.41716	−1.45848	−1.48103	−1.49068
BPANLA	−20.05855	−11.39455	−3.45502	3.56129	9.18633
BPBNLA	2.61663	−11.85500	−27.73692	−45.45337	−65.45543
BPCNLA	17.44193	23.24955	31.19194	41.89209	56.26910
BCANLA	−18.38717	−9.59161	−1.55934	5.52201	11.19378
BCBNLA	−0.40325	−15.07434	−31.09017	−48.89502	−68.95335
BCCNLA	18.79045	24.66671	32.65042	43.37312	57.75978

Simulation 7, 3C Fixed (LHS), Table 7 of 8.

Scenario: Official intervention to maintain exchange rates.

Variable	Period 1	Period 2	Period 3	Period 4	Period 5
BTANLB	−2.00566	−2.16353	−2.27482	−2.35288	−2.40895
BTBNLB	3.62385	3.86322	4.02392	4.12999	4.19753
BTCNLB	−1.61823	−1.70060	−1.75019	−1.77725	−1.78883
BPANLB	−24.07031	−13.67351	−4.14604	4.27356	11.02364
BPBNLB	3.13996	−14.22606	−33.28444	−54.54427	−78.54683
BPCNLB	20.93036	27.89957	37.43048	50.27071	67.52319
BCANLB	−22.06465	−11.50998	−1.87122	6.62644	13.43259
BCBNLB	−0.48390	−18.08928	−37.30835	−58.67425	−82.74436
BCCNLB	22.54859	29.60017	39.18067	52.04795	69.31202

Simulation 7, 3C Fixed (LHS), Table 8 of 8.

Scenario: Official intervention to maintain exchange rates.

Variable	Period 1	Period 2	Period 3	Period 4	Period 5
BTANLC	−2.50707	−2.70439	−2.84350	−2.94107	−3.01116
BTBNLC	4.52980	4.82898	5.02985	5.16244	5.24686
BTCNLC	−2.02278	−2.12573	−2.18771	−2.22154	−2.23601
BPANLC	−30.08776	−17.09174	−5.18251	5.34190	13.77942
BPBNLC	3.92493	−17.78241	−41.60517	−68.17972	−98.18265
BPCNLC	26.16283	34.87415	46.78768	62.83782	84.40323
BCANLC	−27.58069	−14.38735	−2.33900	8.28297	16.79059
BCBNLC	−0.60487	−22.61140	−46.63502	−73.34216	−103.42952
BCCNLC	28.18561	36.99988	48.97539	65.05936	86.63924

Simulation 8, 3C Fixed (LHS), Table 1 of 8.

Scenario: Smaller devaluation during Period 3 to catch up with the free market exchange rates of Simulation 6.

Variable	Period 1	Period 2	Period 3	Period 4	Period 5	Period 6
MSA	2010.00000	2040.00000	2075.00000	2115.00000	2160.00000	2210.00000
MLTOTA	30.00000	35.00000	40.00000	45.00000	50.00000	0.00000
DSA	800.00000	781.26995	764.67786	755.39560	744.10217	734.46991
SUNA	1.30697	1.34674	1.37845	1.31612	1.62611	0.00000
INVRLA	18.15796	19.67435	20.11178	21.30764	21.74839	0.00000
QA	63.06968	63.46740	63.78455	63.16123	66.26108	0.00000
FUNA	9214.27983	9027.52298	8955.99503	8707.50486	9060.82088	0.00000
PA	0.10000	0.09838	0.09837	0.09810	0.09919	0.10017
ILTA	39.80100	38.29755	36.85195	35.71610	34.44917	33.23393
PDOTEA	-1.62140	-0.01199	-0.26862	1.10646	0.99162	0.00000
PAVGA	0.09919	0.09837	0.09823	0.09864	0.09968	0.00000
SAVNLA	2.08449	2.22882	2.31313	2.44404	2.52690	0.00000
BDELA	-47.97406	-44.16573	-25.58536	-32.19618	-28.46741	0.00000
ILTAVA	39.04203	37.56779	36.27958	35.07692	33.83610	0.00000
DSDELA	-18.73005	-16.59209	-9.28226	-11.29343	-9.63226	0.00000
ISTA	43.72670	42.22027	40.03214	39.39378	38.10580	0.00000
RLTA	42.10509	38.31412	37.22055	34.23089	33.12904	0.00000
SURA	21.01600	22.65692	23.54700	24.77640	25.35044	0.00000
FURA	40200.01438	41472.45045	42189.04432	43118.15218	43553.65563	44124.29570
MLNFXA	50.05855	46.39455	27.89849	34.64022	30.99431	0.00000
MLFXA	-20.05855	-11.39455	12.10151	10.35978	19.00569	0.00000

Simulation 8, 3C Fixed (LHS), Table 2 of 8.

Scenario: Smaller devaluation during Period 3 to catch up with the free market exchange rates of Simulation 6.

Variable	Period 1	Period 2	Period 3	Period 4	Period 5	Period 6
MSB	2025.00000	2075.00000	2120.00000	2160.00000	2195.00000	2225.00000
MLTOTB	50.00000	45.00000	40.00000	35.00000	30.00000	0.00000
DSB	790.00000	773.04733	752.44291	742.11687	718.02754	690.62828
SUNB	48.92544	52.81724	54.90864	58.25738	59.02978	0.00000
INVRLB	18.47886	20.09130	20.17311	21.84523	22.43645	0.00000
QB	539.25454	578.17260	599.08663	632.57401	640.29798	0.00000
FUNB	78783.37471	82238.54085	84117.80980	87207.62976	87557.05702	0.00000
PB	0.12000	0.11805	0.11804	0.11668	0.11798	0.11915
ILTB	39.01235	37.25529	35.49259	34.35726	32.71196	31.03947
PDOTEB	-1.62100	-0.01199	-1.14880	1.10646	0.99162	0.00000
PAVGB	0.11902	0.11805	0.11736	0.11733	0.11856	0.00000
SAVNLB	2.39250	2.56331	2.65025	2.79888	2.87057	0.00000
BDELB	-44.46754	-56.66275	-29.57027	-71.85586	-85.98612	0.00000
ILTAVB	38.12370	36.36326	34.92031	33.52452	31.86475	0.00000
DSDELB	-16.95267	-20.60442	-10.32603	-24.08933	-27.39926	0.00000
ISTB	43.72860	42.22169	38.79707	39.38693	38.10022	0.00000
RLTB	41.30286	37.27175	37.06721	32.88692	31.40888	0.00000
SURB	20.10112	21.71420	22.58208	23.85512	24.21216	0.00000
FURB	33750.01542	35153.18135	35919.84481	37022.89587	37211.07798	37349.29368
MLNFXB	46.86004	59.22606	32.22052	74.65474	88.85669	0.00000
MLFXB	3.13996	-14.22606	7.77948	-39.65474	-58.85669	0.00000

Simulation 8, 3C Fixed (LHS), Table 3 of 8.

Scenario: Smaller devaluation during Period 3 to catch up with the free market exchange rates of Simulation 6.

Variable	Period 1	Period 2	Period 3	Period 4	Period 5	Period 6
MSC	2040.00000	2080.00000	2120.00000	2160.00000	2200.00000	2240.00000
MLTOTC	40.00000	40.00000	40.00000	40.00000	40.00000	0.00000
DSC	840.00000	835.16721	833.96977	808.59852	807.80573	811.28297
SUNC	4.00250	4.52632	4.80784	4.20556	4.37642	0.00000
INVRLC	17.59841	18.93237	20.81295	20.62756	20.84959	0.00000
QC	90.02502	95.26322	98.07847	92.05561	93.76428	0.00000
FUNC	13152.36927	13550.12082	13771.20756	12690.92876	12821.72469	0.00000
PC	0.15000	0.14757	0.14755	0.15177	0.15344	0.15497
ILTC	41.17647	40.15227	39.33820	37.43512	36.71844	36.21799
PDOTEC	-1.62191	-0.01199	2.85719	1.10646	0.99162	0.00000
PAVGC	0.14878	0.14756	0.14964	0.15260	0.15420	0.00000
SAVNLC	1.95164	2.11291	2.23953	2.31155	2.38548	0.00000
BDELC	-11.88552	-3.01293	-66.11426	-2.13834	9.53522	0.00000
ILTAVC	40.66115	39.74315	38.37486	37.07505	36.46736	0.00000
DSDELC	-4.83279	-1.19744	-25.37126	-0.79279	3.47724	0.00000
ISTC	43.72726	42.22169	44.42187	39.38693	38.10022	0.00000
RLTC	43.50398	40.16907	35.46763	35.93109	35.37602	0.00000
SURC	13.11778	14.31918	14.96585	15.14753	15.46970	0.00000
FURC	27200.00432	28190.56330	28736.13379	28465.02561	28674.87947	28909.56718
MLNFXC	13.83717	5.12585	68.35379	4.44989	-7.14974	0.00000
MLFXC	26.16283	34.87415	-28.35379	35.55011	47.14974	0.00000

Simulation 8, 3C Fixed (LHS), Table 4 of 8.

Scenario: Smaller devaluation during Period 3 to catch up with the free market exchange rates of Simulation 6.

Variable	Period 1	Period 2	Period 3	Period 4	Period 5	Period 6
RST	46.09682	42.23874	40.41009	37.86154	36.74423	0.00000
K	0.83333	0.83333	0.83333	0.84075	0.84075	0.84075
H	0.66667	0.66667	0.66667	0.64641	0.64641	0.64641
KDOTE	-0.00132	-0.00100	0.88984	0.00492	0.00404	0.00000
HDOTE	-0.00039	-0.00100	-3.03952	0.00492	0.00404	0.00000
KAVG	0.83333	0.83333	0.83703	0.84075	0.84075	0.00000
HAVG	0.66667	0.66667	0.65646	0.64641	0.64641	0.00000

Simulation 8, 3C Fixed (LHS), Table 5 of 8.

Scenario: Smaller devaluation during Period 3 to catch up with the free market exchange rates of Simulation 6.

Variable	Period 1	Period 2	Period 3	Period 4	Period 5
BTARL	-16.85100	-18.32761	-18.73333	-19.99152	-20.12228
BTBRL	30.44658	32.72594	34.73553	36.41215	36.59333
BTCRL	-13.59591	-14.40605	-16.00510	-16.42201	-16.47317
BPARL	-202.23182	-115.83044	123.18990	105.02213	190.66980
BPBRL	26.38101	-120.51112	66.28697	-337.98105	-496.43327
BPCRL	175.85081	236.34157	-189.47687	232.95892	305.76347
BCARL	-185.38082	-97.50283	141.92323	125.01365	210.79208
BCBRL	-4.06557	-153.23706	31.55144	-374.39319	-533.02660
BCCRL	189.44672	250.74762	-173.47177	249.38092	322.23664

Simulation 8, 3C Fixed (LHS), Table 6 of 8.

Scenario: Smaller devaluation during Period 3 to catch up with the free market exchange rates of Simulation 6.

Variable	Period 1	Period 2	Period 3	Period 4	Period 5
BTANLA	-1.67138	-1.80294	-1.84026	-1.97204	-2.00576
BTBNLA	3.01987	3.21934	3.41223	3.59183	3.64757
BTCNLA	-1.34852	-1.41716	-1.57225	-1.61993	-1.64202
BPANLA	-20.05855	-11.39455	12.10151	10.35978	19.00569
BPBNLA	2.61663	-11.85500	6.51167	-33.33973	-49.48376
BPCNLA	17.44193	23.24955	-18.61318	22.97995	30.47807
BCANLA	-18.38717	-9.59161	13.94177	12.33182	21.01145
BCBNLA	-0.40325	-15.07434	3.09944	-36.93156	-53.13133
BCCNLA	18.79045	24.66671	-17.04092	24.59988	32.12009

Simulation 8, 3C Fixed (LHS), Table 7 of 8.

Scenario: Smaller devaluation during Period 3 to catch up with the free market exchange rates of Simulation 6.

Variable	Period 1	Period 2	Period 3	Period 4	Period 5
BTANLB	-2.00566	-2.16353	-2.19855	-2.34557	-2.38568
BTBNLB	3.62385	3.86322	4.07658	4.27218	4.33847
BTCNLB	-1.61823	-1.70060	-1.87837	-1.92677	-1.95304
BPANLB	-24.07031	-13.67351	14.45764	12.32207	22.60564
BPBNLB	3.13996	-14.22606	7.77948	-39.65474	-58.85669
BPCNLB	20.93036	27.89957	-22.23712	27.33268	36.25105
BCANLB	-22.06465	-11.50998	16.65620	14.66764	24.99132
BCBNLB	-0.48390	-18.08928	3.70290	-43.92692	-63.19516
BCCNLB	22.54859	29.60017	-20.35875	29.25944	38.20409

Simulation 8, 3C Fixed (LHS), Table 8 of 8.

Scenario: Smaller devaluation during Period 3 to catch up with the free market exchange rates of Simulation 6.

Variable	Period 1	Period 2	Period 3	Period 4	Period 5
BTANLC	−2.50707	−2.70439	−2.80330	−3.05076	−3.10292
BTBNLC	4.52980	4.82898	5.19791	5.55658	5.64281
BTCNLC	−2.02278	−2.12573	−2.39504	−2.50604	−2.54022
BPANLC	−30.08776	−17.09174	18.43444	16.02664	29.40192
BPBNLC	3.92493	−17.78241	9.91935	−51.57675	−76.55166
BPCNLC	26.16283	34.87415	−28.35379	35.55011	47.14974
BCANLC	−27.58069	−14.38735	21.23774	19.07739	32.50484
BCBNLC	−0.60487	−22.61140	4.72144	−57.13333	−82.19448
BCCNLC	28.18561	36.99988	−25.95874	38.05615	49.68996

Simulation 9, 3C Fixed (LHS), Table 1 of 8.

Scenario: Larger devaluation during Period 3 to anticipate the free market exchange rates of Simulation 6.

Variable	Period 1	Period 2	Period 3	Period 4	Period 5	Period 6
MSA	*2010.00000*	2040.00000	2075.00000	2115.00000	2160.00000	2210.00000
MLTOTA	*30.00000*	*35.00000*	*40.00000*	*45.00000*	*50.00000*	0.00000
DSA	*800.00000*	781.26995	764.67786	740.93979	725.31069	710.32930
SUNA	1.30697	1.34674	1.37687	−0.41035	−0.12659	0.00000
INVRLA	18.15796	19.67435	20.87290	21.58044	22.08737	0.00000
QA	63.06968	63.46740	63.76869	45.89654	48.73410	0.00000
FUNA	9214.27983	9027.52298	8955.99503	6325.56534	6662.19014	0.00000
PA	*0.10000*	0.09838	0.09837	0.09948	0.10059	0.10157
ILTA	39.80100	38.29755	36.85195	35.03261	33.57920	32.14160
PDOTEA	−1.62140	−0.01199	1.13377	1.11099	0.98096	0.00000
PAVGA	0.09919	0.09837	0.09892	0.10003	0.10108	0.00000
SAVNLA	2.08449	2.22882	2.32860	2.43596	2.51854	0.00000
BDELA	−47.97406	−44.16573	−66.06614	−45.56827	−45.60194	0.00000
ILTAVA	39.04203	37.56779	35.93077	34.29821	32.85254	0.00000
DSDELA	−18.73005	−16.59209	−23.73807	−15.62910	−14.98139	0.00000
ISTA	43.72670	42.22027	42.04519	39.36094	38.05191	0.00000
RLTA	42.10509	38.31412	35.31776	33.54890	32.28157	0.00000
SURA	21.01600	22.65692	23.53953	24.35149	24.91640	0.00000
FURA	40200.01438	41472.45045	42189.04432	42520.24608	42947.78587	43515.08129
MLNFXA	50.05855	46.39455	68.39474	48.00422	48.12047	0.00000
MLFXA	−20.05855	−11.39455	−28.39474	−3.00422	1.87953	0.00000

Simulation 9, 3C Fixed (LHS), Table 2 of 8.

Scenario: Larger devaluation during Period 3 to anticipate the free market exchange rates of Simulation 6.

Variable	Period 1	Period 2	Period 3	Period 4	Period 5	Period 6
MSB	2025.00000	2075.00000	2120.00000	2160.00000	2195.00000	2225.00000
MLTOTB	50.00000	45.00000	40.00000	35.00000	30.00000	0.00000
DSB	790.00000	773.04733	752.44291	770.94740	755.76756	739.37162
SUNB	48.92544	52.81724	54.89374	60.85062	61.65564	0.00000
INVRLB	18.47886	20.09130	18.58937	21.31958	21.74983	0.00000
QB	539.25454	578.17260	598.93761	658.50644	666.55661	0.00000
FUNB	78783.37471	82238.54085	84117.80980	90756.84912	91121.55709	0.00000
PB	0.12000	0.11805	0.11804	0.11341	0.11467	0.11579
ILTB	39.01235	37.25529	35.49259	35.69201	34.43132	33.23019
PDOTEB	-1.62100	-0.01199	-3.92407	1.11099	0.98096	0.00000
PAVGB	0.11902	0.11805	0.11570	0.11404	0.11523	0.00000
SAVNLB	2.39250	2.56331	2.61204	2.80972	2.88132	0.00000
BDELB	-44.46754	-56.66275	51.99037	-43.30169	-48.47224	0.00000
ILTAVB	38.12370	36.36326	35.59216	35.05600	33.82542	0.00000
DSDELB	-16.95267	-20.60442	18.50449	-15.17984	-16.39594	0.00000
ISTB	43.72860	42.22169	34.93387	39.35346	38.04593	0.00000
RLTB	41.30286	37.27175	41.02657	34.20105	33.12541	0.00000
SURB	20.10112	21.71420	22.57572	24.63874	25.00502	0.00000
FURB	33750.01542	35153.18135	35919.84481	38092.34823	38284.25054	38430.50912
MLNFXB	46.86004	59.22606	-49.37832	46.11141	51.35356	0.00000
MLFXB	3.13996	-14.22606	89.37832	-11.11141	-21.35356	0.00000

Simulation 9, 3C Fixed (LHS), Table 3 of 8.

Scenario: Larger devaluation during Period 3 to anticipate the free market exchange rates of Simulation 6.

Variable	Period 1	Period 2	Period 3	Period 4	Period 5	Period 6
MSC	2040.00000	2080.00000	2120.00000	2160.00000	2200.00000	2240.00000
MLTOTC	40.00000	40.00000	40.00000	40.00000	40.00000	0.00000
DSC	840.00000	835.16721	833.96977	791.84144	785.34689	781.27884
SUNC	4.00250	4.52632	4.80540	3.39524	3.55425	0.00000
INVRLC	17.59841	18.93237	21.62139	20.93691	21.24825	0.00000
QC	90.02502	95.26322	98.05408	83.95244	85.54252	0.00000
FUNC	13152.36927	13550.12082	13771.20756	11570.51569	11694.08196	0.00000
PC	0.15000	0.14757	0.14755	0.15406	0.15578	0.15730
ILTC	41.17647	40.15227	39.33820	36.65933	35.69759	34.87852
PDOTEC	-1.62191	-0.01199	4.41500	1.11099	0.98096	0.00000
PAVGC	0.14878	0.14756	0.15077	0.15492	0.15654	0.00000
SAVNLC	1.95164	2.11291	2.25565	2.29979	2.37340	0.00000
BDELC	-11.88552	-3.01293	-110.93659	-17.95302	-11.52889	0.00000
ILTAVC	40.66115	39.74315	37.97515	36.17526	35.28568	0.00000
DSDELC	-4.83279	-1.19744	-42.12833	-6.49455	-4.06805	0.00000
ISTC	43.72726	42.22169	46.64567	39.35346	38.04593	0.00000
RLTC	43.50398	40.16907	33.44654	35.15773	34.37938	0.00000
SURC	13.11778	14.31918	14.96076	14.84528	15.16187	0.00000
FURC	27200.00432	28190.56330	28736.13379	28040.34483	28245.80198	28479.98427
MLNFXC	13.83717	5.12585	113.19224	20.25281	13.90229	0.00000
MLFXC	26.16283	34.87415	-73.19224	19.74719	26.09771	0.00000

Simulation 9, 3C Fixed (LHS), Table 4 of 8.

Scenario: Larger devaluation during Period 3 to anticipate the free market exchange rates of Simulation 6.

Variable	Period 1	Period 2	Period 3	Period 4	Period 5	Period 6
RST	46.09682	42.23874	40.44503	37.82226	36.70490	0.00000
K	0.83333	0.83333	0.83333	0.87720	0.87720	0.87720
H	0.66667	0.66667	0.66667	0.64572	0.64572	0.64572
KDOTE	-0.00132	-0.00100	5.27023	0.00537	0.00434	0.00000
HDOTE	-0.00039	-0.00100	-3.13714	0.00537	0.00434	0.00000
KAVG	0.83333	0.83333	0.85498	0.87720	0.87720	0.00000
HAVG	0.66667	0.66667	0.65611	0.64572	0.64572	0.00000

Simulation 9, 3C Fixed (LHS), Table 5 of 8.

Scenario: Larger devaluation during Period 3 to anticipate the free market exchange rates of Simulation 6.

Variable	Period 1	Period 2	Period 3	Period 4	Period 5
BTARL	-16.85100	-18.32761	-19.49603	-21.99079	-22.21397
BTBRL	30.44658	32.72594	36.30437	39.53104	39.90580
BTCRL	-13.59591	-14.40605	-16.81598	-17.54167	-17.69400
BPARL	-202.23182	-115.83044	-287.03933	-30.03227	18.59457
BPBRL	26.38101	-120.51112	772.49112	-97.43705	-185.31311
BPCRL	175.85081	236.34157	-485.45179	127.46931	166.71854
BCARL	-185.38082	-97.50283	-267.54330	-8.04148	40.80854
BCBRL	-4.06557	-153.23706	736.18676	-136.96809	-225.21892
BCCRL	189.44672	250.74762	-468.63581	145.01098	184.41254

Simulation 9, 3C Fixed (LHS), Table 6 of 8.

Scenario: Larger devaluation during Period 3 to anticipate the free market exchange rates of Simulation 6.

Variable	Period 1	Period 2	Period 3	Period 4	Period 5
BTANLA	− 1.67138	− 1.80294	− 1.92860	− 2.19981	− 2.24537
BTBNLA	3.01987	3.21934	3.59133	3.95441	4.03366
BTCNLA	− 1.34852	− 1.41716	− 1.66348	− 1.75475	− 1.78850
BPANLA	− 20.05855	− 11.39455	− 28.39474	− 3.00422	1.87953
BPBNLA	2.61663	− 11.85500	76.41700	− 9.74693	− 18.73134
BPCNLA	17.44193	23.24955	− 48.02226	12.75115	16.85181
BCANLA	− 18.38717	− 9.59161	− 26.46614	− 0.80441	4.12490
BCBNLA	− 0.40325	− 15.07434	72.82567	− 13.70134	− 22.76500
BCCNLA	18.79045	24.66671	− 46.35878	14.50590	18.64031

Simulation 9, 3C Fixed (LHS), Table 7 of 8.

Scenario: Larger devaluation during Period 3 to anticipate the free market exchange rates of Simulation 6.

Variable	Period 1	Period 2	Period 3	Period 4	Period 5
BTANLB	− 2.00566	− 2.16353	− 2.25572	− 2.50776	− 2.55971
BTBNLB	3.62385	3.86322	4.20047	4.50799	4.59833
BTCNLB	− 1.61823	− 1.70060	− 1.94563	− 2.00040	− 2.03887
BPANLB	− 24.07031	− 13.67351	− 33.21086	− 3.42478	2.14265
BPBNLB	3.13996	− 14.22606	89.37832	− 11.11141	− 21.35356
BPCNLB	20.93036	27.89957	− 56.16746	14.53620	19.21091
BCANLB	− 22.06465	− 11.50998	− 30.95514	− 0.91702	4.70235
BCBNLB	− 0.48390	− 18.08928	85.17786	− 15.61941	− 25.95189
BCCNLB	22.54859	29.60017	− 54.22183	16.53659	21.24979

Simulation 9, 3C Fixed (LHS), Table 8 of 8.

Scenario: Larger devaluation during Period 3 to anticipate the free market exchange rates of Simulation 6.

Variable	Period 1	Period 2	Period 3	Period 4	Period 5
BTANLC	−2.50707	−2.70439	−2.93944	−3.40675	−3.47732
BTBNLC	4.52980	4.82898	5.47366	6.12404	6.24676
BTCNLC	−2.02278	−2.12573	−2.53537	−2.71751	−2.76978
BPANLC	−30.08776	−17.09174	−43.27732	−4.65251	2.91075
BPBNLC	3.92493	−17.78241	116.46957	−15.09467	−29.00846
BPCNLC	26.16283	34.87415	−73.19224	19.74719	26.09771
BCANLC	−27.58069	−14.38735	−40.33788	−1.24576	6.38807
BCBNLC	−0.60487	−22.61140	110.99591	−21.21871	−35.25522
BCCNLC	28.18561	36.99988	−70.65688	22.46469	28.86749

4. 3C Checklist

This section lists conditions for the solutions of the 3C model that are necessary for equilibrium and/or desirable for realism.

The checklist for the 3C model (with fixed and/or with flexible exchange rates) follows:

MSA > 0.
DSA > 0.
ILTA > 0.
PA > 0.
MSNXTA > 0.
DSNXTA > 0.
ILTNXA > 0.
PNXTA > 0.
INVRLA > 0.
SUNA > 0.
SURA > 0.
FUNA > 0.
FURA > 0.
QA > 0.
PAVGA > 0.
ILTAVA > 0.
ISTA > 0.

MSB > 0.
DSB > 0.
ILTB > 0.
PB > 0.
MSNXTB > 0.
DSNXTB > 0.
ILTNXB > 0.
PNXTB > 0.
INVRLB > 0.
SUNB > 0.
SURB > 0.
FUNB > 0.
FURB > 0.
QB > 0.
PAVGB > 0.
ILTAVB > 0.

ISTB > 0.

MSC > 0.
DSC > 0.
ILTC > 0.
PC > 0.
MSNXTC > 0.
DSNXTC > 0.
ILTNXC > 0.
PNXTC > 0.
INVRLC > 0.
SUNC > 0.
SURC > 0.
FUNC > 0.
FURC > 0.
QC > 0.
PAVGC > 0.
ILTAVC > 0.
ISTC > 0.

K > 0.
H > 0.
KNXT > 0.
HNXT > 0.
KAVG > 0.
HAVG > 0.

(Note: the following three equations are for the model with floating or flexible exchange rates.)

MSNXTA = MSDELA + MSA.
MSNXTB = MSDELB + MSB.
MSNXTC = MSDELC + MSC.

(Note: the following three equations are for the model with fixed exchange rates.)

MSNXTA = MLTOTA + MSA.
MSNXTB = MLTOTB + MSB.
MSNXTC = MLTOTC + MSC.

PNXTA = PA * (1 + (PDOTA/100)).
PNXTB = PB * (1 + (PDOTB/100)).
PNXTC = PC * (1 + (PDOTC/100)).

ILTA = (DSA/MSA) * (THETA/(1 − THETA)) * 100.
ILTB = (DSB/MSB) * (THETA/(1 − THETA)) * 100.
ILTC = (DSC/MSC) * (THETA/(1 − THETA)) * 100.

FURA = (MSA/PA) + ((100 * DSA)/(ILTA * PA)).
FURB = (MSB/PB) + ((100 * DSB)/(ILTB * PB)).
FURC = (MSC/PC) + ((100 * DSC)/(ILTC * PC)).

(Note: The coefficients in the next three equations are elements of the currency preference inverse matrix defined earlier.)

FUNA
       = (10/7) * FURA + (− 10/7) * FURB + 0.0 * FURC.
FUNB
       = (− 1/3) * FURA + 3.0 * FURB + (− 1/3) * FURC.
FUNC
    = (− 2/21) * FURA + (− 4/7) * FURB + (4/3) * FURC.

(Note: The coefficients in the next three equations are elements of the currency preference matrix defined earlier.)

FURA = .80 * FUNA + .40 * FUNB + .10 * FUNC.
FURB = .10 * FUNA + .40 * FUNB + .10 * FUNC.
FURC = .10 * FUNA + .20 * FUNB + .80 * FUNC.

QA = FUNA/(RST + 100).
QB = FUNB/(RST + 100).
QC = FUNC/(RST + 100).

Since values of RST are equal in each currency in equilibrium, there is no need to add A, B, or C at the end of RST in the formulas.

SUNA = − 5 + .1 * QA.
SUNB = − 5 + .1 * QB.
SUNC = − 5 + .1 * QC.

(Note: The coefficients in the next three equations are elements of the currency preference matrix defined earlier.)

SURA = .80 * SUNA + .40 * SUNB + .10 * SUNC.
SURB = .10 * SUNA + .40 * SUNB + .10 * SUNC.
SURC = .10 * SUNA + .20 * SUNB + .80 * SUNC.

PAVGA = DSQRT(PA * PNXTA).
PAVGB = DSQRT(PB * PNXTB).
PAVGC = DSQRT(PC * PNXTC).

SAVNLA = SURA * PAVGA.
SAVNLB = SURB * PAVGB.
SAVNLC = SURC * PAVGC.

BDELA = SAVNLA − MSDELA.
BDELB = SAVNLB − MSDELB.
BDELC = SAVNLC − MSDELC.

ILTAVA = DSQRT(ILTA * ILTNXA).
ILTAVB = DSQRT(ILTB * ILTNXB).
ILTAVC = DSQRT(ILTC * ILTNXC).

DSDELA = (ILTAVA/100) * BDELA.
DSDELB = (ILTAVB/100) * BDELB.
DSDELC = (ILTAVC/100) * BDELC.

DSNXTA = DSA + DSDELA.
DSNXTB = DSB + DSDELB.
DSNXTC = DSC + DSDELC.

ISTA = ILTA + ((ILTA/ILTNXA) − 1) * 100.
ISTB = ILTB + ((ILTB/ILTNXB) − 1) * 100.
ISTC = ILTC + ((ILTC/ILTNXC) − 1) * 100.

PDOTEA = ((100 + ISTA)/(100 + RST)) * 100 − 100.
PDOTEB = ((100 + ISTB)/(100 + RST)) * 100 − 100.
PDOTEC = ((100 + ISTC)/(100 + RST)) * 100 − 100.

PDOTA = PDOTEA.
PDOTB = PDOTEB.
PDOTC = PDOTEC.

RLTA = ((100 + ILTA)/(100 + PDOTEA)) * 100 − 100.
RLTB = ((100 + ILTB)/(100 + PDOTEB)) * 100 − 100.
RLTC = ((100 + ILTC)/(100 + PDOTEC)) * 100 − 100.

INVRLA = 35 − .4 ∗ RLTA.
INVRLB = 35 − .4 ∗ RLTB.
INVRLC = 35 − .4 ∗ RLTC.

The assumption that real investment by country is a function of the real long-term interest rate by currency requires the assumption that businesses of a given country confine their examination of the real long-term interest rate to their own country's currency.

KDOTE = ((100 + ISTA)/(100 + ISTB)) ∗ 100 − 100.
HDOTE = ((100 + ISTA)/(100 + ISTC)) ∗ 100 − 100.

KDOT = ((100 + PDOTA)/(100 + PDOTB)) ∗ 100 − 100.
HDOT = ((100 + PDOTA)/(100 + PDOTC)) ∗ 100 − 100.

KDOT = KDOTE.
HDOT = HDOTE.

KNXT = K ∗ (1 + (KDOT/100)).
HNXT = H ∗ (1 + (HDOT/100)).

K = PA/PB.
H = PA/PC.

KNXT = PNXTA/PNXTB.
HNXT = PNXTA/PNXTC.

KAVG = DSQRT(K ∗ KNXT).
HAVG = DSQRT(H ∗ HNXT).

BPANLA = MLFXA.
BPBNLB = MLFXB.
BPCNLC = MLFXC.

MLFXA + KAVG ∗ MLFXB + HAVG ∗ MLFXC = 0.0

(Note: For floating or flexible exchange rates MLFXA = 0.0,

MLFXB = 0.0, MLFXC = 0.0.)
MLNFXA + MLFXA = MLTOTA.
MLNFXB + MLFXB = MLTOTB.
MLNFXC + MLFXC = MLTOTC.

MLNFXA + BDELA = SAVNLA.
MLNFXB + BDELB = SAVNLB.
MLNFXC + BDELC = SAVNLC.

BTARL = −INVRLA + SUNA.
BTBRL = −INVRLB + SUNB.
BTCRL = −INVRLC + SUNC.

BTARL + BTBRL + BTCRL = 0.0
BPARL + BPBRL + BPCRL = 0.0
BCARL + BCBRL + BCCRL = 0.0

BTANLA = BTARL * PAVGA.
BTBNLA = BTBRL * PAVGA.
BTCNLA = BTCRL * PAVGA.

BTANLB = BTARL * PAVGB.
BTBNLB = BTBRL * PAVGB.
BTCNLB = BTCRL * PAVGB.

BTANLC = BTARL * PAVGC.
BTBNLC = BTBRL * PAVGC.
BTCNLC = BTCRL * PAVGC.

BPARL = BPANLA/PAVGA.
BPBRL = BPBNLB/PAVGB.
BPCRL = BPCNLC/PAVGC.

BPANLB = BPARL * PAVGB.
BPANLC = BPARL * PAVGC.

BPBNLA = BPBRL * PAVGA.
BPBNLC = BPBRL * PAVGC.

BPCNLA = BPCRL * PAVGA.
BPCNLB = BPCRL * PAVGB.

BPARL = BTARL + BCARL.
BPBRL = BTBRL + BCBRL.
BPCRL = BTCRL + BCCRL.

BPANLA = BTANLA + BCANLA.
BPBNLA = BTBNLA + BCBNLA.
BPCNLA = BTCNLA + BCCNLA.

BPANLB = BTANLB + BCANLB.
BPBNLB = BTBNLB + BCBNLB.
BPCNLB = BTCNLB + BCCNLB.

BPANLC = BTANLC + BCANLC.
BPBNLC = BTBNLC + BCBNLC.
BPCNLC = BTCNLC + BCCNLC.

5. 3C Questions and Issues

This section lists some questions about the macroeconomy that can be addressed by the 3C model. Note that the programs used for simulating the 3C model use as control variables MSDELA, MSDELB, and MSDELC (for the floating exchange rate simulation) and MLTOTA, MLTOTB, MLTOTC, KNXT, and HNXT (for the fixed exchange rate simulations). Some of the questions posed below would require programs using ISTA, ISTB, and ISTC, or ILTNXA, ILTNXB, and ILTNXC instead of the money supply changes.

What is the effect of raising MSDEL in one currency under flexible exchange rates? Under fixed exchange rates?

Does higher MSDEL cause lower BP, BT, KNXT, HNXT? Higher P, ILTNXT, IST, RLT, RST? Does it improve BT by lowering KNXT or HNXT?

What is the effect of raising IST in one currency under flexible exchange rates? Under fixed exchange rates?

What is the effect of raising ILTNXT in one currency under flexible exchange rates? Under fixed exchange rates?

What is the effect of a change in the exchange rate (or MSDEL, or IST, or ILTNXT in different currencies) on the balance of payments? On the balance of trade? On P? On the interest rates (ILT, IST, RLT, RST)?

Does it matter whether the change in the exchange rate occurred under floating exchange rates or fixed exchange rates?

What are the effects of changing the currency preference matrix (and its inverse)? Would making both matrices the identity matrix of order three in Simulations 6–9 yield more symmetric solutions? (Note: Such a preference matrix would correspond to each country acquiring and holding only money and perpetual bonds denominated in its own currency.)

7

The 1C(F) Fiscal Model: Theory and Simulation Results

1. 1C(F) Fiscal Extension

The third model is a one-country, one-currency model with fiscal policy. (The variables in the 1C(F) model are listed and defined in Section 3.)

The fiscal policy of the model involves real government purchases, real (net) tax revenues, and government debt service payments.

Control variables in the fiscal model include:

SPNDRL = real government purchases.

TAXRL = real tax revenues (net of transfer payments, see below).

MSDEL = total nominal money growth during the period.

MLDEF = money printed to finance the government budget deficit during the period.

The variable TAXRL represents real (net) tax revenues, that is, net of transfer payments, such as unemployment, social security, and payments to the needy.

In the real world, the size of the government budget deficit or surplus is related to the level of real output and the price level as well as to the particular tax, transfer, and spending programs in place. Both the level of real tax revenues and the level of real transfer payments depend on the rate of real output. When real output declines, real tax revenues fall and real transfer payments rise, causing, *ceteris paribus*, the real government budget deficit to rise (or the real government budget surplus to fall). However, in the model the time paths of real government purchases and real (net) tax revenues are specified in advance.

While limited, the fiscal model can analyze debt service payments, the build-up of government debt, the crowding out of private investment, the increase in private saving due to cuts in real (net) tax revenues, and, to the extent that real government purchases and real (net) tax revenues both change in the same direction by the same amount, the "balanced budget" multiplier properties of the economy. (Note that the government deficit would also include a debt service term.)

In this closed-economy model, domestic real output produced during the period by the nation's producers goes to domestic consumers, domestic investors, and domestic government purchases.

That is,

$$Q = C + INVRL + SPNDRL,$$

where the variables represent real physical flows of production, consumption, investment, and government purchases, respectively.

Domestic income from production equals:

$$Q = C + SAVRL + TAXRL,$$

where the variables represent real physical flows of income, consumption, saving from production, and taxes, respectively.

Noting that production equals income and solving these two equations for Q − C and equating the results, it follows that:

SAVRL = INVRL + SPNDRL − TAXRL.

Notice the following definition.

SAVRL = real saving from production.

In this model, the concept of saving must be examined more carefully than in the two previous models. Saving is related to the acquisition of money and bonds issued for both capital formation and the government budget deficit. On the one hand, saving is the act of abstaining from consuming real (i.e., physical) output which has been newly produced, so that others may invest that portion of the output. On the other hand, saving is also the acquisition of newly issued financial assets. When investors issue financial assets which they give to savers in return for real output, the real value of the newly issued financial assets exactly equals the real value of the physical goods which the savers forgo consuming. But when the public receives interest and dividend payments on its holdings of government debt, the acquisition of the new financial assets has nothing to do with output nor with forgoing consumption. Therefore, the acquisition of the new financial assets is increased by that amount above what it would otherwise be.

That is,

SAVNL = SAVRL * PAVG + GDSNL

The model assumes that GDSNL, nominal government debt service payments to the public, are an addition to saving over and above the amount saved from production and that all of the debt service payments are saved. (This assumption may be extreme, but it seems reasonable to believe that a higher proportion of the debt service payments is saved than of disposable income.)

In the 1C(F) model the linking equation is:

MSDEL + BDEL = (SAVRL * PAVG) + GDSNL

(where SAVRL means real saving from production, and both sides of the equation equal SAVNL, total nominal saving).

From this it follows that:

$$\text{SAVNL} = \text{INVNL} + \text{SPNDNL} - \text{TAXNL} + \text{GDSNL}$$

or

$$\text{SAVNL} = \text{INVNL} + \text{DEFNL}.$$

where:

$$\text{INVNL} = \text{INVRL} * \text{PAVG},$$
$$\text{SPNDNL} = \text{SPNDRL} * \text{PAVG},$$
$$\text{TAXNL} = \text{TAXRL} * \text{PAVG},$$
$$\text{DEFNL} = \text{SPNDNL} - \text{TAXNL} + \text{GDSNL},$$

and where

$$\text{DEFNL} = \text{nominal government budget deficit.}$$

The division of after-tax (i.e., disposable) income into saving and consumption is determined as follows:

$$\text{Q} - \text{TAXRL} = \text{C} + \text{SAVRL}$$

where:

$$\text{Q} - \text{TAXRL} = \text{real disposable income,}$$

and this disposable income is divided, by the consumption function, into consumption and saving from production:

$$\text{SAVRL} = -5 + .1 * (\text{Q} - \text{TAXRL}).$$

The nominal debt service payments on government debt held by the public are given by the formula:

$$\text{GDSNL} = (\text{IST}/100) * \text{NDMSAV} + \text{NDDSAV}.$$

This formula is far from perfect, but it seems like the best choice available. The debt service for money is taken to be at rate IST (since there is in the model no "average" short-term nominal interest rate during the period).

2. 1C(F) Simulation Notes

The fiscal simulations attempted to shed light on the current policy questions—namely, the effect of the mix of monetary policy (taken in this case to be the path of MSDEL) and fiscal policy (taken in this case to be the paths of TAXRL and SPNDRL).

Two additional fiscal simulations failed to converge and have been omitted. Both simulations probably failed to converge because the policy variables caused too sudden a decline in the government claim on real saving from production. The difference between the simulations was that one had constant money growth and the other had a modest increase in money growth.

In the 1C world, consistency between the 1C model and the 1C(F) model requires that the 1C(F) model should reproduce the results of the 1C model provided the fiscal variables are all set to zero. This does happen. Note that the requirement in the fiscal model checklist that NDMS and NDDS be positive is not really necessary. The requirement is generally desirable because the geometric means of money debt and perpetual bond debt during the period would be zero if the starting levels of the money debt or perpetual bond debt, respectively, were zero. This would cause nominal debt service to be unrealistically low in those cases.

3. 1C(F) Variables

List of Variable Names for 1C(F) Model
Shown in Simulations 10–12, Table 1

MS = nominal money supply, start of period.
MSDEL = change in nominal money supply during period.
DS = annual nominal dividend stream from perpetual bonds, start of period.

RLT = real long-term interest rate, start of period.

INVRL = real investment during period.

Q = real output during period.

FADRL = stock demand for real financial assets, start of period.

P = price level, start of period.

ILT = nominal long-term interest rate, start of period.

PDOTE = expected rate of price change during period.

PAVG = price level, average over period.

SAVRL = real saving (from production) during period.

BDEL = nominal principal value of perpetual bonds (net) newly issued during period.

ILTAVG = nominal long-term interest rate, average over period.

DSDEL = change in annual nominal dividend stream from perpetual bonds during period.

IST = nominal short-term interest rate, start of period.

RST = real short-term interest rate, start of period.

List of Variable Names for 1C(F) Model
Not Shown in Simulations 10–12, Table 1

MSNXT = nominal money supply, end of period.

PNXT = price level, end of period.

ILTNXT = nominal long-term interest rate, end of period.

DSNXT = annual nominal dividend stream from perpetual bonds, end of period.

PDOT = actual rate of price change realized during period.

List of Variable Names for 1C(F) Model
Shown in Simulations 10–12, Table 2

SPNDRL = real government purchases of goods during period.

TAXRL = real net taxes (tax revenues less transfer payments) during period.

GDSRL = real government outlays for debt service during the period.

GDSNL = nominal government outlays for debt service during the period.

DEFRL = real government deficit during the period.

DEFNL = nominal government deficit during the period.

INVNL = nominal investment during period.

SAVNL = nominal (total) saving during period.

MLDEF = money created during the period to finance the deficit.

BLDEF = nominal principal value of perpetual bonds created during the period to finance the deficit.

DLDEF = annual nominal dividend stream from perpetual bonds created during the period to finance the deficit.

NDMS = nominal short-term government debt, start of period.

NDDS = nominal long-term government debt, start of period.

NDRL = real value of government debt, start of period.

List of Variable Names for 1C(F) Model
Not Shown in Simulations 10–12, Table 2

NDMSNX = nominal short-term government debt, end of period.

NDMSAV = nominal short-term government debt, average over period.

NDDSNX = nominal long-term government debt, end of period.

NDDSAV = nominal long-term government debt, average over period.

NDRLNX = real value of government debt, end of period.

4. Tables for 1C(F) Simulations 10–12

This section contains tables for Simulations 10–12, numerical examples of the 1C(F) model. In the simulation tables the values in italics are exogenous.

Simulation 10, 1C Fiscal (LHS), Table 1 of 2.

Scenario: Constant government claim on real saving from production; constant money growth. (See Simulation 11.)

Variable	Period 1	Period 2	Period 3	Period 4	Period 5	Period 6
MS	*2010.00000*	2040.00000	2070.00000	2100.00000	2130.00000	2160.00000
MSDEL	*30.00000*	*30.00000*	*30.00000*	*30.00000*	*30.00000*	0.00000
DS	*800.00000*	793.22551	788.87265	787.51136	790.23144	798.71708
RLT	54.97289	38.00365	35.74827	35.53106	34.38937	0.00000
INVRL	13.01085	19.79854	20.70069	20.78758	21.24425	0.00000
Q	255.10855	322.98553	332.00704	332.87587	337.44265	0.00000
FADRL	40200.01438	45227.83287	45602.17351	45472.02869	45461.00925	45189.80404
P	*0.10000*	0.09021	0.09079	0.09236	0.09371	0.09560
ILT	39.80100	38.88360	38.10979	37.50054	37.10007	36.97764
PDOTE	−9.79003	0.63763	1.73963	1.45316	2.01705	0.00000
PAVG	0.09498	0.09050	0.09157	0.09303	0.09465	0.00000
SAVRL	18.01085	24.79854	25.70069	25.78758	26.24425	0.00000
BDEL	−17.22052	−11.30767	−3.60093	7.29249	22.91013	0.00000
ILTAVG	39.33963	38.49475	37.80394	37.29977	37.03880	0.00000
DSDEL	−6.77449	−4.35286	−1.36129	2.72008	8.48564	0.00000
IST	42.16032	40.91409	39.73443	38.57998	37.43115	0.00000
RST	57.58620	40.02358	37.34711	36.59717	34.71597	0.00000

Simulation 10, 1C Fiscal (LHS), Table 2 of 2.

Scenario: Constant government claim on real saving from production; constant money growth. (See Simulation 11.)

Variable	Period 1	Period 2	Period 3	Period 4	Period 5	Period 6
SPNDRL	*30.00000*	*30.00000*	*30.00000*	*30.00000*	*30.00000*	0.00000
TAXRL	*25.00000*	*25.00000*	*25.00000*	*25.00000*	*25.00000*	0.00000
GDSRL	116.53826	181.75702	262.59362	375.07156	532.79227	0.00000
GDSNL	11.06883	16.44814	24.04562	34.89339	50.42619	0.00000
DEFRL	121.53826	186.75703	267.59362	380.07155	537.79227	0.00000
DEFNL	11.54374	16.90061	24.50347	35.35854	50.89941	0.00000
INVNL	1.23577	1.79167	1.89556	1.93389	2.01066	0.00000
SAVNL	12.77948	18.69233	26.39907	37.29249	52.91013	0.00000
MLDEF	*1.00000*	*1.00000*	*1.00000*	*1.00000*	*1.00000*	0.00000
BLDEF	10.54374	15.90061	23.50347	34.35854	49.89941	0.00000
DLDEF	4.14787	6.12090	8.88524	12.81566	18.48214	0.00000
NDMS	*18.00000*	19.00000	20.00000	21.00000	22.00000	23.00000
NDMSAV	18.49324	19.49359	20.49390	21.49419	22.49444	0.00000
NDDS	*1.80000*	5.94787	12.06877	20.95400	33.76966	52.25180
NDDSAV	3.27203	8.47251	15.90248	26.60093	42.00625	0.00000
NDRL	225.22506	380.18639	569.12850	832.31713	1206.13788	1718.74473
NDNL	22.52250	34.29659	51.66841	76.87653	113.02317	164.30647

Simulation 11, 1C Fiscal (LHS), Table 1 of 2.

Scenario: Constant government claim on real saving from production; modest increase in money growth.
(See Simulations 10 and 12.)

Variable	Period 1	Period 2	Period 3	Period 4	Period 5	Period 6
MS	2010.00000	2040.00000	2075.00000	2115.00000	2160.00000	2210.00000
MSDEL	30.00000	35.00000	40.00000	45.00000	50.00000	0.00000
DS	800.00000	793.22551	786.99178	781.96191	779.18839	780.11109
RLT	54.97289	38.66926	35.67039	34.99259	33.02581	0.00000
INVRL	13.01085	19.53230	20.73185	21.00297	21.78968	0.00000
Q	255.10855	320.32307	332.31857	335.02976	342.89687	0.00000
FADRL	40200.01438	45227.83287	45932.80203	46052.15835	46352.25658	46363.01337
P	0.10000	0.09021	0.09035	0.09185	0.09320	0.09533
ILT	39.80100	38.88360	37.92731	36.97219	36.07354	35.29914
PDOTE	-9.79003	0.15457	1.66354	1.46645	2.29108	0.00000
PAVG	0.09498	0.09028	0.09110	0.09252	0.09426	0.00000
SAVRL	18.01085	24.53230	25.73185	26.00297	26.78968	0.00000
BDEL	-17.22052	-16.23263	-13.43208	-7.59450	2.58572	0.00000
ILTAVG	39.33963	38.40248	37.44671	36.52010	35.68424	0.00000
DSDEL	-6.77449	-6.23373	-5.02987	-2.77352	0.92270	0.00000
IST	42.16032	41.40498	40.51066	39.46338	38.26734	0.00000
RST	57.58620	41.18866	38.21339	37.45005	35.17246	0.00000

Simulation 11, 1C Fiscal (LHS), Table 2 of 2.

Scenario: Constant government claim on real saving from production; modest increase in money growth. (See Simulations 10 and 12.)

Variable	Period 1	Period 2	Period 3	Period 4	Period 5	Period 6
SPNDRL	30.00000	30.00000	30.00000	30.00000	30.00000	0.00000
TAXRL	25.00000	25.00000	25.00000	25.00000	25.00000	0.00000
GDSRL	116.53826	183.35136	265.91478	378.28668	531.09457	0.00000
GDSNL	11.06883	16.55261	24.22381	34.99962	50.06050	0.00000
DEFRL	121.53826	188.35136	270.91478	383.28668	536.09457	0.00000
DEFNL	11.54374	17.00400	24.67929	35.46222	50.53180	0.00000
INVNL	1.23577	1.76334	1.88859	1.94322	2.05388	0.00000
SAVNL	12.77948	18.76737	26.56792	37.40550	52.58572	0.00000
MLDEF	1.00000	1.00000	1.00000	1.00000	1.00000	0.00000
BLDEF	10.54374	16.00400	23.67929	34.46222	49.53180	0.00000
DLDEF	4.14787	6.14593	8.86711	12.58564	17.67504	0.00000
NDMS	18.00000	19.00000	20.00000	21.00000	22.00000	23.00000
NDMSAV	18.49324	19.49359	20.49390	21.49419	22.49444	0.00000
NDDS	1.80000	5.94787	12.09380	20.96091	33.54655	51.22159
NDDSAV	3.27203	8.48129	15.92159	26.51728	41.45248	0.00000
NDRL	225.22506	380.18639	574.29036	845.85423	1233.85953	1763.33838
NDNL	22.52250	34.29659	51.88678	77.69372	114.99490	168.10718

Simulation 12, 1C Fiscal (LHS), Table 1 of 2.

Scenario: Declining government claim on real saving from production; modest increase in money growth. (See Simulation 11.)

Variable	Period 1	Period 2	Period 3	Period 4	Period 5	Period 6
MS	2010.00000	2040.00000	2075.00000	2115.00000	2160.00000	2210.00000
MSDEL	30.00000	35.00000	40.00000	45.00000	50.00000	0.00000
DS	800.00000	793.22551	787.09762	782.06833	779.28130	780.06351
RLT	54.97289	29.66026	32.08306	28.08464	28.16720	0.00000
INVRL	13.01085	23.13590	22.16678	23.76614	23.73312	0.00000
Q	255.10855	342.60907	319.16787	321.41155	307.33132	0.00000
FADRL	40200.01438	45227.83287	42948.66126	41920.13629	40032.68817	38578.27126
P	0.10000	0.09021	0.09663	0.10091	0.10791	0.11457
ILT	39.80100	38.88360	37.93242	36.97723	36.07784	35.29699
PDOTE	−9.79003	7.11347	4.42854	6.94274	6.17213	0.00000
PAVG	0.09498	0.09336	0.09874	0.10435	0.11119	0.00000
SAVRL	18.01085	26.88590	24.66678	25.01614	23.73312	0.00000
BDEL	−17.22052	−15.95595	−13.42870	−7.63054	2.19199	0.00000
ILTAVG	39.33963	38.40506	37.45178	36.52476	35.68528	0.00000
DSDEL	−6.77449	−6.12789	−5.02929	−2.78704	0.78222	0.00000
IST	42.16032	41.39119	40.51560	39.47014	38.29006	0.00000
RST	57.58620	32.00350	34.55865	30.41806	30.25287	0.00000

Simulation 12, 1C Fiscal (LHS), Table 2 of 2.

Scenario: Declining government claim on real saving from production; modest increase in money growth. (See Simulation 11.)

Variable	Period 1	Period 2	Period 3	Period 4	Period 5	Period 6
SPNDRL	30.00000	27.50000	25.00000	22.50000	20.00000	0.00000
TAXRL	25.00000	23.75000	22.50000	21.25000	20.00000	0.00000
GDSRL	116.53826	177.09575	244.43221	333.10751	445.66133	0.00000
GDSNL	11.06883	16.53389	24.13562	34.75902	49.55305	0.00000
DEFRL	121.53826	180.84574	246.93220	334.35751	445.66133	0.00000
DEFNL	11.54374	16.88399	24.38247	34.88946	49.55305	0.00000
INVNL	1.23577	2.16000	2.18878	2.47994	2.63888	0.00000
SAVNL	12.77948	19.04405	26.57130	37.36946	52.19199	0.00000
MLDEF	1.00000	1.00000	1.00000	1.00000	1.00000	0.00000
BLDEF	10.54374	15.88399	23.38247	33.88946	48.55305	0.00000
DLDEF	4.14787	6.10026	8.75715	12.37804	17.32629	0.00000
NDMS	18.00000	19.00000	20.00000	21.00000	22.00000	23.00000
NDMSAV	18.49324	19.49359	20.49390	21.49419	22.49444	0.00000
NDDS	1.80000	5.94787	12.04812	20.80527	33.18332	50.50961
NDDSAV	3.27203	8.46526	15.83239	26.27524	40.93991	0.00000
NDRL	225.22506	380.18639	535.68964	765.71243	1056.20514	1449.73043
NDNL	22.52250	34.29659	51.76208	77.26510	113.97701	166.09890

5. 1C(F) Checklist

This section lists conditions for the solutions of the 1C(F) model that are necessary for equilibrium and/or desirable for realism.
  The checklist for the 1C(F) model follows:

MS > 0.
DS > 0.
ILT > 0.
P > 0.
MSNXT > 0.
DSNXT > 0.
ILTNXT > 0.
PNXT > 0.
INVRL > 0.
SAVRL > 0.
FADRL > 0.
Q > 0.
PAVG > 0.
ILTAVG > 0.
IST > 0.
NDMS > 0.
NDMSNX > 0.
NDMSAV > 0.
NDDS > 0.
NDDSNX > 0.
NDDSAV > 0.
NDRL > 0.
NDNL > 0.
NDRLNX > 0.
NDNLNX > 0.
ILT = ((DS * THETA)/(MS * (1 − THETA))) * 100.
MSNXT = MSDEL + MS.
NDMSNX = NDMS + MLDEF.
NDMSAV = DSQRT(NDMS * NDMSNX).
FADRL = MS/(P * THETA).
Q = FADRL/(RST + 100).
SAVRL = − 5 + .1 * (Q − TAXRL).
SPNDNL = PAVG * SPNDRL.
TAXNL = PAVG * TAXRL.

BLDEF = DEFNL − MLDEF.
DLDEF = (ILTAVG/100) * BLDEF.
NDDSNX = NDDS + DLDEF.
NDDSAV = DSQRT(NDDS * NDDSNX).
GDSNL = (IST/100) * NDMSAV + NDDSAV.
GDSRL = GDSNL/PAVG.
DEFNL = SPNDNL − TAXNL + GDSNL.
DEFRL = DEFNL/PAVG.
INVRL = SAVRL − SPNDRL + TAXRL.
INVNL = PAVG * INVRL.
INVRL = 35 − .4 * RLT.
PDOTE = ((100 + ILT)/(100 + RLT)) * 100 − 100.
PDOT = PDOTE.
PNXT = P * (1 + (PDOT/100)).
PAVG = DSQRT(P * PNXT).
SAVNL = SAVRL * PAVG + GDSNL.
SAVNL = MSDEL + BDEL.
ILTAVG = DSQRT(ILT * ILTNXT).
DSDEL = (ILTAVG/100) * BDEL.
DSNXT = DS + DSDEL.
IST = ILT + ((ILT/ILTNXT) − 1) * 100.
RST = ((100 + IST)/(100 + PDOTE)) * 100. − 100.
NDRL = (NDMS + (NDDS/(ILT/100)))/P.
NDNL = NDMS + (NDDS/(ILT/100)).
NDRLNX
    = (NDMSNX + (NDDSNX/(ILTNXT/100)))/PNXT.
NDNLNX = NDMSNX + (NDDSNX/(ILTNXT/100)).

6. 1C(F) Questions and Issues

This section lists some questions about the macroeconomy that can be addressed by the 1C(F) model.

What is the effect of changing the proportion of government purchases financed by taxes, by printing money, by printing perpetual bonds? What is the effect of changing the proportion of the deficit financed by printing money or printing perpetual bonds?

How do lower real government purchases and/or higher real (net) tax revenues affect the economy?

The model uses real tax revenues rather than the average or marginal tax rates. For certain purposes it might be useful to analyze the effects of particular constant values of the average or marginal tax rates. In this case it is not enough to keep real tax revenues unchanged. If real tax revenues were kept unchanged, but if real output varied, then the average tax rate would be changed. To simulate an unchanged average tax rate would require varying real tax revenues to correspond with real output. If and only if real tax revenues were a one-to-one function of the average or marginal tax rates would it be possible to adjust real tax revenues to simulate particular constant values of the average or marginal tax rates, respectively. The same remarks apply to real saving and to the average and marginal saving rates.

(Note: Because neither the average nor marginal tax rate is an explicit variable in the present model, the next three questions would require modifications to the model.)

How will cuts in tax rates affect real (net) tax revenues? The deficit?

Do cuts in tax rates increase saving enough so that the increased deficit, if one is created by the tax cut, will not raise interest rates?

Will cuts in real (net) tax revenues increase real saving? Real investment? Real output? Inflation?

To what extent will the impetus from increased government purchases boost real output and, therefore, real (net) tax revenues and, thereby, reduce future deficits? The total amount of money and perpetual bonds created to finance the deficit depends on the time paths of government purchases and government revenues, which, together with the time-path of government debt service payments, define the deficit. The longer the lag and the smaller the induced response in government revenues, the larger the deficit (and the required financing) will be.

Does a large deficit and fast monetary growth cause inflation? A balance of payments deficit (under fixed exchange rates)? Currency depreciation (under flexible or floating exchange rates)? Higher interest rates? Lower real output?

Does a combination of a larger deficit and a slower growth in the money supply depress real output? Slow inflation? Raise interest rates? (Some people argue that the inflationary premium in nominal interest rates will be reduced.)

Others argue that the higher interest rates in this situation increase saving—a classical view.

Given the low saving rate, will larger budget deficits raise interest rates? Crowd out investment? Forestall economic recovery?

It is sometimes claimed that budget deficits are not a danger to the economy provided that the central bank allows the money supply to grow enough so that the government can borrow without causing large increases in interest rates.

Alternatively, it is claimed that such an expansion of the money supply would, by raising expectations of inflation, cause nominal interest rates to rise.

Would a combination of a smaller deficit (or a budget surplus) and a faster growth of the money supply boost real output? Increase real investment? Lower interest rates?

Do government budget deficits cause inflation? What is the effect of having a deficit of a given amount with different relative amounts of government purchases, government (net) tax revenues, and government debt service payments? Does a large difference between the amount of government purchases and government (net) tax revenues cause inflation? What is the effect of having such a difference of a given amount but with different amounts of government purchases and government (net) tax revenues?

What is the effect on PDOTE, Q, and other variables of lower MSDEL? Higher IST? Higher ILTNXT? Higher RST? Higher RLT? (The preceding control variables can be considered to represent alternative definitions of a restrictive monetary policy.)

What is the effect on Q, PDOTE, and other variables of higher SPNDRL? Lower TAXRL? Higher SPNDRL − TAXRL? Higher SPNDRL − TAXRL + GDSRL? (The preceding expressions, when treated as control variables, can be considered to represent alternative definitions of a stimulative fiscal policy. Note: The present model does not treat GDSRL as a control variable.)

What is the effect on various economic variables of different combinations of values of the monetary and fiscal variables mentioned above? How would the effect of each such combination be affected by changes in MLDEF?

8

Concluding Remarks

1. Limitations of the Analysis

This section mentions, and discusses briefly, some of the limitations of the analysis.

Because the model is an equilibrium model, it cannot handle unexpected events such as "overnight" devaluations or "sudden" money-bond operations.

Because the model has deterministic (rather than stochastic) relationships, it cannot handle risk or uncertainty.

Because the model has only a single type of good, it cannot be used to study relative prices between different types of goods (e.g., tradables vs. nontradables).

The model does not contain gold, gold-backed money or bonds, or purchasing-power-indexed money or bonds.

The model has no labor supply schedule, no labor market, and no unemployment. Instead, real output determines (employment which determines) real wages.

The 3C model, in addition to omitting all fiscal variables, also omits domestic and international payments of interest and dividends, as well as any flows necessary to finance them. This is an important omission, especially as international indebtedness rises. In an extended 3C model, with debt service and a fiscal sector, it would be useful to trace all flows of money and bonds in each currency, within the private sector, between the government and the public, and between countries.

Because the fiscal model has no explicit marginal tax rates, it cannot analyze "supply-side" effects (i.e., tax or other incentives to working, employing, or producing). The present fiscal model can only specify an implicit average (net) tax rate of Q/TAXRL, which glosses over any incentive impacts from marginal tax rates on the level of real output. To allow for an explicit analysis of possible increases in tax revenues following reductions in tax rates (by means of increases in the tax base), SPNDRL and TAXRL could be changed to make them functions of real output, the average price level, and a tax rate variable. A still more realistic fiscal sector would likely split real (net) tax revenues into a tax revenue component and a transfer payment component, where the tax revenue component would have real tax revenues increasing with increases in the price level as well as in proportion to real output and where the transfer component would have real transfer outlays rising as real output fell.

The model's financial sector is extremely limited. The financial process of the model has investors issuing money and perpetual bonds directly to savers in return for real output. There are no explicit financial intermediary institutions, domestic or international.

The model lacks an explicit aggregate balance sheet. Each financial instrument created in the model's simplified financial process is both an asset (to its buyer, the saver) and a liability (to its issuer, the investor). Ideally, a model would consider assets and liabilities, both short-term and long-term, in each currency. However, the model looks at money and bonds only as financial assets of their holders, not as financial liabilities of their issuers. Actual and potential holders of financial assets regard money and bonds as uniform "commodities" and are indifferent to the identity of the original issuer. The lack of forced repayment makes the omission of the liability side less pressing, but means that there is no real credit, in the sense of repayable lending, in the model.

The model also lacks an explicit aggregate income statement, except for the case of the government sector budget in the 1C(F) model, which has (net) tax receipts, outlays for purchases, and debt service payments.

Many issues arise in connection with the treatment of time in the model. For example, the model has no explicit subjective discount rate of time preference. However, the portfolio preference indifference curves implicitly embody time preferences, since they compare perpetual dividend streams with money.

In another time-related matter, because the model's time horizon is limited to the end of the current period, the public cannot respond rationally in the present to changes in government policy or economic conditions which are expected to occur in the future (for example, to a credibly-promised future tax cut or to a confidently-expected future decline in the real long-term interest rate).

Because the model has no way to define a "long-term price level" it cannot define either an actual or an expected "long-term inflation rate." The lack of an adequate expected long-term inflation rate means that the variable RLT in the model is an artificial construct which is a necessary compromise.

A related limitation to the one-period time horizon is that the model contains no financial assets with finite maturities, at least of more than a single period. For some purposes, money can be considered to mature every period. With this interpretation, money can be considered to be a short-term asset.

The model's treatment of expectations over its one-period horizon also raises questions. Because of the absence of financial claims with multiperiod maturities there are no liquidity pressures as repayment dates draw near. And because the model is an equilibrium model, there is no possibility that the expectations might be wrong. Whatever adjustment takes place in the model is not to wrong expectations but to changing correct expectations. In other words, the model inhabits a world of dynamic equilibrium rather than a world of dynamic disequilibrium. In such a circumstance, it naturally comes as no surprise that the model contains no explicit method of forming expectations and no discussion of the degree of confidence placed in the expectations.

The fact that the model is a deterministic equilibrium model makes it impossible to analyze such real world phenomena as the slowdown in the growth of bank lending caused by bankers' reactions to spreading bankruptcies among heavily indebted firms. The model also cannot represent or analyze the consequences to the economy of the failure to repay an obligation in a timely manner, nor of credit crunches, liquidity crises, disintermediation, illiquidity, insolvency, bankruptcy, default, repudiation, rescheduling of debts, or refunding to longer maturity.

The model has no real possibility of bankruptcy. In fact it is not clear if (or how) bankruptcy could be handled in a deterministic equilibrium model, since it generally is unexpected by outsiders. Perhaps foreclosure and/or liquidation could occur whenever net worth (i.e., equity) became zero, whether or not loan repayments were due.

Although the model cannot simulate bankruptcy, it can simulate a large decline in the nominal money supply, which might accompany widespread bankruptcies. Also, Section 6 of Chapter 2 discusses the reaction of IST to changes in ILT, such as might occur during periods of monetary tightening or loosening.

Because the model does not explicitly include a variable for the capital stock, as well as because it is (1) deterministic, (2) in equilibrium, and (3) without multiperiod financial liabilities which must come due, the present model cannot be used to analyze borrowing against accumulated equity in real assets. In a more general model overextended lending might trigger bankruptcies and a serious economic decline.

A more fundamental question about the model concerns the use of a period or discrete time structure of time in the model instead of continuous time. Certainly, a change in the length of the time period in the model would not affect the underlying economic relationships which the model is intended to portray, but might it not affect the simulations? I have not attempted to change the length of the time period and re-solve the model, but my reflections lead me to believe that if the length of the time period were changed, the variables in the model would respond in natural ways, except perhaps for RLT. Of course, it is likely that altered values of RLT would cause altered values in all the remaining variables also. If the length of the time period were to approach zero, the present discrete time model would tend toward the limiting case of a continuous time model. In such a limiting case, I believe that the difficulty with RLT would disappear. Another way to stabilize RLT as the length of the time period is changed—other than by resorting to a continuous time model—would be to redefine RLT so that the expectation of inflation (i.e., PDOTE in the definition of RLT) extended over a fixed amount of real time, instead of only until the end of the period, no matter what the length.

A technical question concerns the model's reliance on the geometric mean for computing various averages. Three of the equations in the model—the linking equation, the equation relating the nominal principal value of new bond issues to the change in the annual nominal dividend stream, and the foreign exchange equation—may be "pseudo-equilibrium" conditions, in the sense that there is no reason to believe that the average values during the period—for the price level (i.e., PAVG), the nominal long-term interest rate (i.e., ILTAVG), and the foreign exchange rates (i.e., KAVG and HAVG), respectively—which are required to satisfy these equations are those defined by the geometric mean. Nevertheless, it may well be that the equations (and the simulations) are not very sensitive to the exact specifications.

2. Epilogue

The theory introduced in this book represents an attempt to demystify macroeconomics and to return that subject to the realm of consistency and common sense.

The theory in this book is a dynamic equilibrium theory which takes special pains to distinguish between real and nominal, physical and financial, supply and demand, stock and flow, expectations and actual realizations, and long-term and short-term concepts.

For me the major lesson of Post Keynesian Macrodynamics is that there may well be more constraints on the macroeconomic process than is usually recognized. If so, other frameworks may have more "give" or "play" in them than actually exists. For a given set of initial conditions, it appears that the range of policy actions consistent with equilibrium is small.

Finally, the world of Post Keynesian Macrodynamics, however compelling, is not an empirically-derived world. The empirical and policy relevance of the model, and any necessary or desirable modifications to the framework presented here, may best be determined by a cautious and skeptical economics profession.

The comments and suggestions of thoughtful readers will prove an invaluable aid in improving the book and are welcome. All comments and suggestions become the property of Michael A. Salant, who may use or distribute whatever information you supply in any way he believes appropriate.

Appendices

Appendix 1 Programs

The twelve simulations were generated by seven different programs, which can be described briefly as follows:

Programs 1 (RHS, for Simulation 1) **and 2** (LHS, for Simulations 2 and 3) 1C model.
Initial variables (start of period 1):
MS, DS, P.
Control variable (during each period):
MSDEL.
Output variables (end of each period):
MSNXT, DSNXT, PNXT.

Program 3 (LHS, Simulation 4) 1C model.
Initial variables (start of period 1):
MS, DS, P.
Control variable (end of each period):
ILTNXT.
Output variables (end of each period):
MSNXT, DSNXT, PNXT.
Note: Presumably, the same 1C LHS (or RHS) solution may be generated by programs having different control variables. For example: MSDEL, ILTNXT, or IST.

Program 4 (Simulation 5) 1C model.
Initial variables (start of period 1):
MS, DS, P.
Control variable (during each period):
Q.
Output variables (end of each period):
MSNXT, DSNXT, PNXT.
Note: In the descriptions of the next two programs the names of the currency variables lack the final A, B, or C.

Program 5 (Simulation 6) 3C model (floating exchange rates).
Initial variables (start of period 1):
In each currency: MS, DS, P.
Control variables (during each period):
In each currency: MSDEL.
Output variables (end of each period):
In each currency: MSNXT, DSNXT, PNXT.

Program 6 (Simulations 7–9) 3C model (fixed exchange rates).
Initial variables (start of period 1):
In each currency: MS, DS, P.
Control variables (during each period):
In each currency: MLTOT.
Also: KNXT, HNXT.
Output variables (end of each period):
In each currency: MSNXT, DSNXT, PNXT.

Program 7 (LHS, Simulation 10–12) 1C(F) model.
Initial variables (start of period 1):
MS, DS, P, NDMS, NDDS.
Control variables (during each period):
MSDEL, MLDEF, SPNDRL, TAXRL.
Output variables (end of each period):
MSNXT, DSNXT, PNXT, NDMSNX, NDDSNX.

Appendix 2 Wages

This appendix discusses the inclusion of wage rates in the closed-country model(s) and the international model. In between the closed-country and the international discussions, some necessary notation is introduced.

Wages in the 1C Closed-Country Model

Real and nominal wage rates may be added to the model. If one assumes that real output is a function of employment and that employment is a function of the level of real wages, then real output during the period is a function of the average level of real wages during the period. Multiplying the average level of real wages during the period by the average price level during the period, one obtains the average level of nominal wages during the period. (This last statement is true if the average during the period for the price level, real wages, and nominal wages are all computed using the geometric mean.) Thus, the average level of nominal wages during the period is derived indirectly from the value of real output during the period and the average price level during the period. The model provides no way of obtaining the level of nominal wages either at the start of the period or at the end of the period. In addition, the average level of nominal wages during the period does not affect any other variable in the model. (The only variable affected by the average level of real wages during the period is the average level of nominal wages during the period.) If one chooses arbitrarily a particular level of nominal wages at the start of the period, then one can obtain nominal wages at the end of the period, which is the start of the next period. (Note that the level of the nominal wage rate at the end of the period is a function of the level of the nominal wage rate at the start of the period and the average level of the nominal wage rate during the period.) Thus, by choosing nominal wages at the start of the first period, it is possible to obtain the nominal wages at the start (and end) of every period.

In contrast, the standard Keynesian approach begins with an arbitrary value of nominal wages (and the money supply) and simultaneously solves for real output and the price level (and other variables).

Question: Should the model deflate by wages instead of price levels?

Suggested Wage Variables for 1C Model

WNL = nominal wage rate, start of period.
WNLNXT = nominal wage rate, end of period.
WNLVAG = nominal wage rate, average over period.
WRL = real wage rate, start of period.
WRLNXT = real wage rate, end of period.
WRLAVG = real wage rate, average over period.

Suggested Wage Variables for 3C Model

(Note: These names lack the final A, B, or C.)

WNL = nominal wage rate, start of period.
WNLNX = nominal wage rate, end of period.
WNLAV = nominal wage rate, average over period.
WRL = real wage rate, start of period.
WRLNX = real wage rate, end of period.
WRLAV = real wage rate, average over period.

Wages in the 3C International Model

Let us look very briefly at how wages might fit into the international model. If the ratios of the average nominal wages in Currencies A and B and Currencies A and C during the period equal KAVG and HAVG, respectively, then (since the ratios of PAVGA and PAVGB and PAVGA and PAVGC are also equal to KAVG and HAVG, respectively) it follows that

WRLAVA = WRLAVB = WRLAVC, that is, that real wages are equal in each currency. If this is so, real outputs cannot be independent in each country, since the real output in each country is a function of the real wage in that country's currency.

Contrapositively, if the real outputs in the three countries are independent, then real wages are not equalized in each currency (country).

Note: The assumption that real output by country is a function of the average real wage by currency over the period requires the assumption that businesses and workers in a given country pay and are paid only in the currency of that country.

Appendix 3
Geometric Mean

Note that because of the choice of the geometric mean to define PAVGA, PAVGB, PAVGC, KAVG, and HAVG, where:

PAVGA = DSQRT(PA * PNXTA)
PAVGB = DSQRT(PB * PNXTB)
PAVGC = DSQRT(PC * PNXTC)
KAVG = DSQRT(K * KNXT)
HAVG = DSQRT(H * HNXT)

and:

K = PA/PB
KNXT = PNXTA/PNXTB
H = PA/PC
HNXT = PNXTA/PNXTC

it also follows that:

KAVG = PAVGA/PAVGB
HAVG = PAVGA/PAVGC

which is consistent with the spirit of the definitions of K and H as ratios of the price levels in the various currencies.

Also note that because of the choice of the geometric mean to define WNLAVG, PAVG, and WRLAVG, where:

WNLAVG = DSQRT(WNL * WNLNXT)
PAVG = DSQRT(P * PNXT)
WRLAVG = DSQRT(WRL * WRLNXT)

and:

WRL = WNL/P
WRLNXT = WNLNXT/PNXT

it also follows that:

WRLAVG = WNLAVG/PAVG

which is consistent with the spirit of the definition of the real wage as the ratio of the nominal wage to the price level.

The choice of the geometric mean is meant to simplify the examples not to make them rigorous. An alternative measure would give:

PAVG = (PNXT − P)/(DLOG(PNXT/P))
ILTAVG = (ILTNXT − ILT)/(DLOG(ILTNXT/ILT))
KAVG = (KNXT − K)/(DLOG(KNXT/K))
HAVG = (HNXT − H)/(DLOG(HNXT/H))
WNLAVG = (WNLNXT − WNL)/(DLOG(WNLNXT/WNL))
WRLAVG = (WRLNXT − WRL)/(DLOG(WRLNXT/WRL))
NDMSAV = (NDMSNX − NDMS)/(DLOG(NDMSNX/NDMS))
NDDSAV = (NDDSNX − NDDS)/(DLOG(NDDSNX/NDDS))

Appendix 4
More General Portfolio Preferences

In the 1C model the stock demand for real FA's determines the desired total real value of the money-bonds portfolio for each country, and the indifference curves between money and bonds (derived from the utility function) determine the preferred disposition of that total between money and bonds.

In the present 3C model, the disposition of the total portfolio between money and bonds is the same for each combination of country and currency. For all combinations of country and currency, the proportions of money and bonds in the total portfolio held in a particular currency by a particular country is given by the scalars THETA and (1 − THETA), respectively. The value of THETA is 0.50 in the present model.

However, it is possible to construct a more complicated model which would permit the proportion of money to bonds to be different, although still fixed, for each combination of country and currency. In this more complicated model both THETA and (1 − THETA) would be three-by-three matrices, and there would have to be a separate portfolio preference utility function for each combination of country and currency. (In order for the necessary inverse matrices to exist, it is necessary that no two countries have the same currency preferences for either money or bonds.)

In the generalized version, each of the three countries would have a portfolio preference utility function (between money and perpetual bonds) for each of the three currencies, for a total of nine such functions in all.

For any country I and currency J,
THETA(I,J) = the proportion of money in Currency J to total FA's in Currency J in the portfolio of Country I.

THETA(I,J) can also be defined using the utility functions as:

THETA(I,J) = B(I,J)/C(I,J), where B(I,J) and C(I,J) are the parameters B and C in the utility function for Country I in Currency J.

In the generalized 3C model the following relationships would exist:

Country A's stock demand for real money in Currency A = (THETA(A,A)) * (Country A's stock demand for real FA's in Currency A).

Country A's stock demand for real money in Currency B = (THETA(A,B)) * (Country A's stock demand for real FA's in Currency B).

Country A's stock demand for real money in Currency C = (THETA(A,C)) * (Country A's stock demand for real FA's in Currency C).

Country A's stock demand for real perpetual bonds in Currency A = (1 − THETA(A,A)) * (Country A's stock demand for real FA's in Currency A).

Country A's stock demand for real perpetual bonds in Currency B = (1 − THETA(A,B)) * (Country A's stock demand for real FA's in Currency B).

Country A's stock demand for real perpetual bonds in Currency C = (1 − THETA(A,C)) * (Country A's stock demand for real FA's in Currency C).

Country B's stock demand for real money in Currency A = (THETA(B,A)) * (Country B's stock demand for real FA's in Currency A).

Country B's stock demand for real money in Currency B = (THETA(B,B)) * (Country B's stock demand for real FA's in Currency B).

Country B's stock demand for real money in Currency C = (THETA(B,C)) * (Country B's stock demand for real FA's in Currency C).

Country B's stock demand for real perpetual bonds in Currency A = (1 − THETA(B,A)) * (Country B's stock demand for real FA's in Currency A).

Country B's stock demand for real perpetual bonds in Currency B = (1 − THETA(B,B)) * (Country B's stock demand for real FA's in Currency B).

Country B's stock demand for real perpetual bonds in Currency C = (1 − THETA(B,C)) * (Country B's stock demand for real FA's in Currency C).

Country C's stock demand for real money in Currency A = (THETA(C,A)) * (Country C's stock demand for real FA's in Currency A).

Country C's stock demand for real money in Currency B = (THETA(C,B)) * (Country C's stock demand for real FA's in Currency B).

Country C's stock demand for real money in Currency C = (THETA(C,C)) * (Country C's stock demand for real FA's in Currency C).

Country C's stock demand for real perpetual bonds in Currency A = (1 − THETA(C,A)) * (Country C's stock demand for real FA's in Currency A).

Country C's stock demand for real perpetual bonds in Currency B = (1 − THETA(C,B)) * (Country C's stock demand for real FA's in Currency B).

Country C's stock demand for real perpetual bonds in Currency C = (1 − THETA(C,C)) * (Country C's stock demand for real FA's in Currency C).

Global stock demand for real money in Currency A
  = Country A's stock demand for real money in Currency A
  + Country B's stock demand for real money in Currency A
  + Country C's stock demand for real money in Currency A.

Global stock demand for real money in Currency B
= Country A's stock demand for real money in Currency B
+ Country B's stock demand for real money in Currency B
+ Country C's stock demand for real money in Currency B.

Global stock demand for real money in Currency C
= Country A's stock demand for real money in Currency C
+ Country B's stock demand for real money in Currency C
+ Country C's stock demand for real money in Currency C.

Global stock demand for real bonds in Currency A
= Country A's stock demand for real bonds in Currency A
+ Country B's stock demand for real bonds in Currency A
+ Country C's stock demand for real bonds in Currency A.

Global stock demand for real bonds in Currency B
= Country A's stock demand for real bonds in Currency B
+ Country B's stock demand for real bonds in Currency B
+ Country C's stock demand for real bonds in Currency B.

Global stock demand for real bonds in Currency C
= Country A's stock demand for real bonds in Currency C
+ Country B's stock demand for real bonds in Currency C
+ Country C's stock demand for real bonds in Currency C.

Appendix 5
International Fiscal

Let us briefly show how the fiscal model could be placed in an international context. Heretofore, it has been assumed that SPNDRL represents domestic government purchases of domestic output, that TAXRL represents (net) domestic government tax revenues levied on domestic income, and that GDSRL represents domestic government debt service payments to domestic holders of domestic government debt.

More generally, the domestic government could purchase foreign output, could tax foreign income (or foreign residents), and could service debts held by foreign holders of its obligations. In addition, foreign governments could purchase domestic output, could tax domestic income (or residents) and could service debts held by domestic residents. Even in this appendix, the words "domestic" and "foreign" must be placed in an international setting, so that "domestic" may refer to each of the three countries in turn and "foreign" may refer to each pair of "non-domestic" countries in turn.

In an international setting, the variables in the fiscal model should be viewed as follows. In the formula

$$DEFNL = SPNDNL - TAXNL + GDSNL,$$

SPNDNL represents purchases by the domestic government from both domestic and foreign production. TAXRL represents payments to the domestic government by both domestic and foreign residents. And GDSNL represents payments by the domestic government to both domestic and foreign holders of its obligations.

In the formulas

$$INVRL = SAVRL - SPNDRL + TAXRL$$

and

$$SAVNL = SAVRL * PAVG + GDSNL,$$

SPNDRL represents purchases of domestic production by both domestic and foreign governments. TAXRL represents payments by domestic residents to both domestic and foreign governments. And GDSNL represents debt service payments to domestic residents from both domestic and foreign governments.

This is only the barest beginning. A thorough treatment would take account of the real flows of government purchases, tax revenues, and debt service payments between the various countries and of the money and perpetual bonds in each currency issued to finance the various budget deficits.

Appendix 6
Adjustment to Portfolio
Disequilibrium

Although the model is a dynamic equilibrium model and cannot be viewed in either a disequilibrium or static framework, it may be helpful for understanding to let old habits of thought assert themselves in order to see how the money-bonds diagram would register adjustment to disequilibrium in a comparative statics framework.

In the money-bonds diagram:

• Increases in the price level, *ceteris paribus*, cause the portfolio point to move radially toward the origin, and decreases in the price level, *ceteris paribus*, cause the portfolio point to move radially away from the origin.

• Increases in the nominal long-term interest rate, *ceteris paribus*, cause the portfolio point to move horizontally leftward toward the real money axis and parallel to the real bond axis, and decreases in the nominal long-term interest rate, *ceteris paribus*, cause the portfolio point to move horizontally rightward away from the real money axis and parallel to the real bond axis.

• Increases in the nominal money supply, *ceteris paribus*, cause the portfolio point to move vertically upward away from the real bond axis and parallel to the real money axis, and decreases in the nominal money supply, *ceteris paribus*, cause the portfolio point to move vertically downward toward the real bond axis and parallel to the real money axis.

• Increases in the annual nominal dividend stream from perpetual bonds, *ceteris paribus*, cause the portfolio point to move horizontally rightward away from the real money axis and parallel to the real bond axis, and decreases in the annual nominal dividend stream from perpetual bonds, *ceteris paribus*, cause the portfolio point to move horizontally leftward toward the real money axis and parallel to the real bond axis.

The determination of the stock demands for real money and real bonds can be thought of as a two-step procedure. One step, the determination of the desired ratio of real money to real bonds, is performed by the utility function. The other step, the determination of the stock supply of real FA's, which functions as a "macro" budget constraint in the process of utility maximization, is performed in equilibrium by the stock demand for real FA's. The steps may be viewed in either order.

The adjustment process by which the stock supplies of real money and real bonds are brought into conformity with the stock demands for real money and real bonds involves changes in the price level, which affects the stock supplies of both real money and real bonds, and changes in the nominal long-term interest rate, which affects only the stock supply of real bonds. Increases in the price level reduce the stock supplies of both real money and real bonds in the same proportion, while increases in the nominal long-term interest rate reduce the stock supply of real bonds, having no effect whatever on the stock supply of real money.

If at any time the actual portfolio position of the public were not equal to the portfolio position that the public demanded, that is, the point of tangency between the highest indifference curve and the real financial asset iso-supply line equal to real financial asset demand, then equilibrating forces would be set up which would change the price level and the nominal long-term interest rate to bring the supply of real money and the supply of real bonds into line with the demand for real money and the demand for real bonds.

These equilibrating forces act as follows:

• If the stock supply of real money exceeds the stock demand for real money, then the price level will rise.

• If the stock supply of real money is less than the stock demand for real money, then the price level will fall.

• If the ratio of the stock supply of real money to the stock supply of real bonds exceeds the ratio of the stock demand for real money to the stock demand for real bonds, then the nominal long-term interest rate will fall.

• If the ratio of the stock supply of real money to the stock supply of real bonds is less than the ratio of the stock demand for real money to the stock demand for real bonds, then the nominal long-term interest rate will rise.

For example, if the public were to find itself with too much real money but exactly the desired stock of real bonds, the public would respond by bidding up the price level until the stock supply of real money equaled the desired stock demand for real money and, since this price level increase would have reduced the supply of real bonds below the desired stock, bidding down the nominal long-term interest rate to increase the supply of real bonds to the stock which is desired.

In the money-bonds diagram, the difference between a central bank policy of keeping the nominal long-term interest rate low and keeping the nominal money supply low can be seen as a central bank attempt to hold the ratio of MS/DS relatively higher in the former case and relatively lower in the latter case. The reaction of the public would produce a relatively greater rise (relatively smaller fall) in the price level and a relatively greater fall (relatively smaller rise) in the nominal long-term interest rate in the former case and a relatively greater fall (relatively smaller rise) in the price level and a relatively greater rise (relatively smaller fall) in the nominal long-term interest rate in in the latter case. Note that this analysis is static. The discussion in the 1C Simulation Notes covers certain dynamic aspects of interest rate policy.

The adjustment process in the 3C model with floating exchange rates can be viewed in three stages: (1) after swapping among the individual economic units; (2) after prices have adjusted in each currency; (3) after nominal long-term interest rates have adjusted in each currency. For example, consider the following table:

The Three Stages of the Adjustment Process

	Real stock supply as percent of real stock demand:		
Item	After swapping	After P adjusts	After ILT adjusts
Real money in Currency A	50	100	100
Real money in Currency B	250	100	100
Real money in Currency C	100	100	100
Real bonds in Currency A	200	400	100
Real bonds in Currency B	100	40	100
Real bonds in Currency C	25	25	100

In the first stage, the different economic units swap, trade, and exchange money and bonds, money and goods, and domestic money and foreign money, until, for each combination of money and bonds in each currency, the ratio of real supply to real demand is the same for every economic unit. In the table, the situation after swapping is shown in the first column of figures.

In the second stage, prices in each currency adjust. For the example, PA would fall to 50 percent of its previous value; PB would rise to 250 percent of its previous value; and PC would remain unchanged. In the table, the situation after prices adjust is shown in the second column of figures. Note that the adjustment of prices, designed to bring the real money stock supply into equality with the real money stock demand, has also affected the real stock supply of bonds.

In the third stage, nominal long-term interest rates adjust to bring the real stock supply of bonds into equality with the real stock demand for bonds. For the example, ILTA would rise to 400 percent of its previous value; ILTB would fall to 40 percent of its previous value; and ILTC would fall to 25 percent of its previous value. In the table, the situation after interest rates adjust is shown in the third column of figures. In the final equilibrium, every economic unit has 100 percent of its desired stock of real money and real bonds in each currency. (Note: In practice, adjustment might occur in simultaneous fashion, rather than in the sequence listed above.)

Appendix 7
Payments of Interest
and Dividends

The extent (if any) to which the nominal money supply, or MSDEL, would or might be affected by the payments of interest and dividends is heavily affected by institutional considerations. Thus, dividends on perpetual bonds might or might not be paid using existing money, but interest payments on money would tend to cause the nominal money supply to increase. Under some circumstances payments of interest and dividends on money and bonds which were originally issued for purposes of capital formation might well net out, being merely a flow of old (i.e., existing) money, not new money, from investors (borrowers) to savers (lenders).

Money and bonds could also have been originally created by the central bank in its money-bond operations or its foreign exchange operations or by the government (that is, the Treasury) in its operations to finance the government budget deficit and/or debt service. Because the central bank can create both money and bonds, it could either (1) create money to pay interest and dividends, or (2) create and sell perpetual bonds and use the money proceeds to pay interest and dividends. In the 1C(F) model, debt service payments on government debt may be financed by printing money or bonds or by levying taxes.

A model which included such matters would first have to determine the amounts of money and bonds outstanding which had originally been issued by the private sector for capital formation purposes and the amounts which had been issued by the central bank during money-bond operations and/or foreign exchange operations.

The model would then have to determine for the money and bonds issued by the private sector whether the payments of interest and dividends would net out or not and for the money and bonds issued by the central bank the amounts of money and/or bonds which the central bank would print to pay interest and dividends.

Once these determinations were made, the model could solve for the amount of the increase (if any) in the nominal money supply due to payments of interest and dividends as well as for the nominal short-term interest rate, the average level of money balances over the period, the average annual nominal dividend stream over the period, and all other variables.

In the course of these rather involved computations, those changes in the nominal money supply and in the annual nominal dividend stream from perpetual bonds which were due to payments of interest and dividends would be separated from those changes which were due to capital formation and other causes. Thus, if the change in the stock supply of nominal money due to payments of interest and dividends were 25, and the value of MSDEL in the model were 60, then the "true" value of MSDEL (i.e., net of the change in MS due to interest and dividend payments) would be 35. This value of 35 would then be treated as MSDEL is treated in the present model. Whereas at present the variable MSDEL can change due to at most four causes (the saving-investment process, money-bond operations, foreign exchange operations, government financial operations), in a model which allowed for interest and dividend payments such payments would constitute a fifth source of monetary expansion.

Payment flows from interest and dividends would be even more complex in an international model, especially one with fiscal policy.

Note: When comparing two simulations which differ in values of control variables other than MSDEL, the value of MSDEL may need to be adjusted for payments of interest and dividends in order to obtain comparable "true" values of MSDEL.

Suggested Readings

Ackley, Gardner. *Macroeconomic Theory*. New York: Macmillan, 1961.

Bailey, Martin J. *National Income and the Price Level; a Study in Macro-Theory*. New York: McGraw-Hill, 1962.

Gurley, John G., and Edward S. Shaw, with a mathematical appendix by Alain C. Enthoven. *Money in a Theory of Finance*. Washington, D.C.: The Brookings Institution, 1960.

Hicks, John Richard. "Mr. Keynes and the 'Classics': a suggested interpretation." *Econometrica*. April 1937.

———. *Value and Capital*, 2nd Edition. London: Oxford University Press, 1965.

Johnson, Harry G. "Towards a General Theory of the Balance of Payments," Chapter 23 in *Readings in International Economics*, edited by Richard E. Caves and Harry G. Johnson. Homewood, Illinois: Richard D. Irwin, 1968.

———. *Macroeconomics and Monetary Theory*. Chicago: Aldine, 1972.

Keynes, John Maynard. *(A Tract on) Monetary Reform*. New York: Harcourt, Brace & Co., 1924.

———. *A Treatise on Money*. New York: Harcourt, Brace & Co., 1930.

———. *The General Theory of Employment, Interest, and Money*. London: Macmillan, 1936.

Laffer, Arthur B. "An Anti-Traditional Theory of the Balance of Payments Under Fixed Exchange Rates," mimeo, February 1969.

Laidler, David E. *Demand for Money: Theories and Evidence*. New York: Harper and Row, 1978.

McKinnon, Ronald I. *Money and Capital in Economic Development*. Washington, D.C.: The Brookings Institution, 1973.

————, and Edward S. Shaw. "Policies in Restraint of Development." Stanford University, 1968, mimeo.

Mundell, Robert A. *International Economics.* New York: Macmillan, 1968.

————. *The Dollar and the Policy Mix: 1971.* Essays in International Finance, No. 85. May 1971, International Finance Section, Department of Economics, Princeton University.

Patinkin, Don. "Financial Intermediaries and the Logical Structure of Monetary Theory," A Review Article. *American Economic Review,* March 1961.

Salant, Walter S. "The Demand for Money and the Concept of Income Velocity." *Journal of Political Economy,* June 1941.

Shaw, Edward S. *Financial Deepening in Economic Development.* New York: Oxford University Press, 1973.

————. "International Inflation: 1958–1973," November 1, 1974. Preliminary draft. Mimeo. Federal Reserve Bank of San Francisco.

————. "International Money and International Inflation: 1958–1973," December 3, 1974. Mimeo. Federal Reserve Bank of San Francisco.

Index

171

Reader's Comments

Your views about this book will help to improve it. All comments and suggestions become the property of Michael A. Salant. Possible topics for comment are:

Usefulness   Clarity   Accuracy   Completeness   Spelling
Graphics   Tables   Typography   Layout   Price   Rigor
Availability   Organization   Legibility   Durability   Redundancy   Length

Please indicate your name and address if you wish a reply. Thank you for your cooperation.

Colophon

The text type is Linotron Baskerville No. 2, 11 points leaded 2 points, and the headings are Linotron Clarendon, 18 points.

The type was set on a Linotron 202 digital CRT photo-typesetter driven by a Data General NOVA computer under the Penta System front end.

The type on a full page is 39 lines deep by 26 picas wide.

The trim size is 6 inches by 9 inches.

Text paper: Spring Forge, white, smooth, 50 lb., 540 PPI, 90.5 opacity, non-acid.

Cover color: PMS 300 with UV coating.

Soft cover paper: Carolina, coated one-side, 10 pt.

Hard cover paper: Pasted oak board covered with B-grade pyroxylin-impregnated cloth, 84 pt.

Binding: Perfect (adhesive).

Press run: 1250 (paperback), 750 (hardbound).

How to Order

Prices: $16.00 paperback, $24.00 hardbound.

Residents of Washington, D.C., please add 6 percent sales tax of 96¢ per copy (paperback) or $1.44 per copy (hardbound), plus $2.95 per copy for surface postage and handling.

If your bookstore or library does not have this book, you may order it by sending your name, address, phone number, the number of copies desired for each type of binding, and a check (in U.S. currency only) for the full amount to:

Michael A. Salant
Post Office Box 33421
Farragut Station
Washington, D.C. 20033-0421

Dealer and book club inquiries are invited.